CARE OF HOUSEPLANTS

ALAN TOOGOOD

AURA
EDITIONS

Editor: Susanne Mitchell
Designer: John Fitzmaurice
Picture research:
   Moira McIlroy

Published by
Aura Editions
2 Derby Road
Greenford, Middlesex

Produced by
Marshall Cavendish Books Ltd
58 Old Compton Street
London W1V 5PA

ISBN 0 86307 448 0

Typeset in Century Old Style
by Quadraset Ltd, Avon

Printed and bound in Italy
by L.E.G.O.

CONTENTS

INTRODUCTION

Opposite Foliage plants are very much part of the decor in this unusual but attractive green and white room

Below Wardian cases were first used by plant collectors to transport plants from foreign parts back to this country. The Victorians used them for growing the more difficult plants and they are still used for this purpose. Nowadays they are often called terrariums, and a typical example is shown here

MILLIONS OF PEOPLE all over the world grow plants in their homes. Often this is for the sheer pleasure of growing and caring for plants, for the human race has a close affinity with plants and nature.

Most of us need greenery around us, for it is the most natural thing in the world. Growing plants indoors puts many people in closer touch with nature, especially city and town dwellers, and particularly those who live in flats and apartments with no gardens.

Houseplants not only satisfy our need for foliage and flowers but also play an important part in 'furnishing' our homes — they add the finishing touches, give the home the appearance of being lived in and contrast with and complement our furnishings and decor.

But houseplants are not only grown in private homes — there is scarcely an hotel, restaurant, airport lounge or office that does not have plants of some kind for the pleasure of customers and workers.

HOUSEPLANT HISTORY

While plants have been grown indoors for centuries, it is really only since mid-Victorian times that indoor cultivation of a wide selection of plants has enjoyed widespread popularity in this country.

In the Victorian era a great many plants were collected by 'plant hunters' in the tropics and sub-tropics and eventually it was discovered that many were suitable for cultivation in the home. Indeed many of the plants that are so popular today were collected in this way during the last century.

Among the most popular plants with the Victorians were ferns, the aspidistra, or cast-iron plant, and palms of various kinds. These succeeded in the poorly lit rooms of Victorian houses.

A structure known as the Wardian case was often used by Victorians for growing the more difficult or delicate plants. This was an enclosed glass case, with a wooden or metal frame, often very ornate, which provided a humid micro-climate for those plants that would not stand normal room conditions. The Wardian case was 'discovered' or invented by Nathaniel Ward in 1834 and, in fact, was used by plant collectors to transport their plants (by ship) back to this country. Before the invention of the

Above Highly ornate Wardian cases of the Victorian era. They were used to grow the more difficult and delicate tropical plants

Wardian case many plants died during the long voyages to Europe; but when transported in these glass containers they arrived fresh.

Unfortunately today Wardian cases are difficult to obtain and the genuine Victorian ones are prized collectors' pieces. There is renewed interest in them, however, for their very decorative effect and one or two companies are manufacturing modern equivalents. The very popular bottle garden works on the same principle.

Fashions in houseplants have changed, though, over the years. In the early part of the twentieth century indoor plants were not so popular, although cacti and succulents were widely grown.

In the 1940s there was renewed interest in growing houseplants and this has increased steadily since then. Today houseplants are more popular then ever before: even those people who have no interest in gardening, and very little in plants, usually have some indoor plants about the house.

Right Poinsettias are now much dwarfer than they used to be due to the action of chemical dwarfing compounds used by the growers. Newer strains flower more freely and come in a wider range of colours

HOUSEPLANTS TODAY

Never before has there been a wider range available: foliage plants, flowering kinds for all seasons, plants for short- and long-term use, and certainly plants for every conceivable place in the home, from the darkest corner to the lightest windowsill, from the unheated room to the warm lounge or sitting room.

Houseplants can be bought from chain stores, florists, nurseries and garden centres, and indeed many garden centres have vast display and sales areas, and include all the sundries and equipment needed for indoor cultivation.

New plants are still being put on the market by houseplant producers even though today very few new species are collected from the wild.

Some producers are looking at the potential use of various tropical and sub-tropical plants at present in botanic garden collections. Often some of these prove to be good houseplants which can be propagated in quantity and sold in many outlets.

Also, plant breeding is producing new cultivars and hybrids of existing plants, particularly the flowering pot plants. Exciting new cultivars of such pot plants as primula, calceolaria and cineraria have appeared on the market. Becoming very popular for winter and spring colour are the new strains of coloured primroses, for instance. There is a new Barberton daisy or gerbera called 'Happipot' which promises to rival the dwarf pot chrysanthemum, with its large daisy flowers in a wide range of colours.

New cultivars of popular foliage plants are appearing as well, such as philodendrons, begonias, and the polka dot plant (*Hypoestes*). There are also new caladium hybrids with attractive, highly coloured paper-thin leaves, but unfortunately these are tricky plants to grow for more than a short time in the average house.

Chemical 'dwarfing' compounds have provided nurserymen with the means to retard the growth of some plants artificially to make them suitable for the home. The dwarf pot chrysanthemum is very well known and highly popular; it must be one of the top-selling houseplants and is available all the year round. Poinsettias, so popular at Christmas time, have also been dwarfed; the new strains are much freer flowering than the old kinds, and come in other colours — pink and white — as well as scarlet.

Above The polka dot plant, or hypoestes, has become very popular in recent years and, as well as being easily grown, is not difficult to raise from seeds in the home

Fashion plays its part, too, in the houseplant popularity ratings as certain groups of plants catch the attention of the gardening public and, as a result, growers make them more readily available. A prime example is the group of plants related to the pineapple and known as bromeliads. These, commonly called the urn and air plants, are grown for their attractive foliage and often spectacular flowers. On the whole they are very easy houseplants and could eventually take over from cacti. The air plants (species of *Tillandsia*) are grown without soil and the best way to display them is to mount them on a piece of driftwood.

Carnivorous plants (the insect eaters) have also become popular as people are finding they make novel and excellent windowsill plants, especially the Venus fly trap and some of the trumpet pitchers (*Sarracenia*).

Houseplants are excellent value for money for they last (even the short-term ones) far longer than cut flowers. Many are easy to grow and there is no reason why every home should not be full of living greenery and colour.

CHAPTER ONE

CHOOSING THE BEST

Opposite Fireplaces make excellent sites for groups of houseplants. In this plastic trough have been grouped a palm, asparagus fern and rubber plant – an excellent contrast in foliage shape

Right An attractive winter arrangement combining the flowers of poinsettia and winter begonia with the foliage of a variegated fatshedera and ivies. This should remain attractive for several months

IT IS VERY tempting to buy houseplants on impulse — how can you really resist one of those beautiful coloured-leaved caladiums or crotons, or at Christmas time a poinsettia, with its rich scarlet, flower-like bracts? Yet you should try to resist the temptation because it is best not to buy a plant unless you are certain that you can provide the right conditions for it and have the time to look after it properly.

If you do not have too much time for looking after plants then draw up a list of easy-going subjects, which do not need much attention, and buy only these. On the other hand, if you have plenty of time for plant care then ease of cultivation

may not be all that important to you.

Make sure you can provide the right temperature for a plant — for instance, a plant that needs a temperature of 21°C (70°F) will not be happy for long if you can only keep it in a cool room, or a room with wildly fluctuating temperatures. You should also consider if you can provide the plant with sufficient humidity, shade or sun as appropriate, and, if necessary, draught-free conditions.

The descriptive plant lists in this book will help you to decide which ones are suitable for your home and then you can buy accordingly.

Also, before you go on a buying trip, try to decide what you want the plant for — you may need a climber to frame an alcove, you may want a large bold specimen to stand in a fireplace, or you may want half-a-dozen plants to form a nice group. It is so much easier to buy plants for a specific purpose.

PICK A HEALTHY PLANT

As with most things we buy today, it is necessary to shop around to obtain the best value, for plants certainly vary in quality. Generally speaking, if you go to a garden centre, florist or chain store which has a good reputation for quality you will not go far wrong, but neverthe-less you should inspect plants thoroughly and the following notes will give you an idea of the things to watch out for.

First, never buy houseplants from an open market stall, or plants which are standing on the pavement outside a shop. Most houseplants are tropical or sub-tropical (coming from warm climates) and they can suffer terribly when placed

out of doors. The plants may look fine but it is when you get them home that trouble can start — leaves may fall for no apparent reason or the plants may simply curl up and die. This is because they have been subjected to cold conditions and draughts on the stall or pavement.

Make sure the plant is well wrapped before you leave the shop or garden centre, especially if the weather is cold, otherwise your tender plant could suffer on the way home, and, again, look decidedly sick a few days later.

Avoid any plants which have been on the shelf of a chain store for a long time — often they look 'tired' and jaded, and maybe the compost has dried out. Try to buy from a chain store the most recently delivered plants which are at the peak of health. This means keeping a close eye on the plant shelves.

If you buy from a garden centre or florist, often it does not matter if the plants have been there for some time, for generally they are well cared for by the staff and are being kept in optimum conditions as regards light, temperature and humidity. Having said that, most flowering plants, of course, have a limited shelf life.

Occasionally one sees mail-order firms offering houseplants — be wary of these for it is generally best to see plants before you buy. However, there are several specialist houseplant producers, and growers of cacti and succulents, African violets, bromeliads, orchids and carnivorous plants, who offer a mail-order service, and these specialists do sell high-quality plants. Their catalogues often make very interesting reading, too, with specialist advice on plant care.

When you buy from a garden centre, florist or chain store, the plants generally have cultivation tags which give such information as temperature needed and light requirements, and although this information is necessarily brief, it will give you an idea about whether or not you can provide the right conditions for the plant.

A word about bonsai — or dwarf trees — which are considered later in this book. The majority of these are hardy trees and only suitable for growing out of doors, so do not consider them as houseplants, even though they may be offered for sale with tender plants. There are one or two exceptions, for sometimes tender trees are dwarfed and can be grown indoors.

How do you know if you are buying a healthy plant? A plant in peak condition should be strong and sturdy, of a uniform colour, with no spindly or weak growth at the top. There should be plenty of buds on flowering plants, with some flowers open.

You should avoid plants with wilting or damaged leaves, and especially any whose leaves have brown dried-up edges, or brown 'scorch' marks. Avoid any plants whose leaves have unnatural-looking brown spots or patches.

Avoid plants that appear far too big for their pots, for this often means that they are pot-bound: the pot is packed full of roots and this results in a severe check to growth. Also avoid plants that are loose in their pots for this indicates that they are not very well rooted, or the roots may be rotting off. Such plants may die rather quickly.

BUYING FLOWERING PLANTS

There are various points to watch out for when buying some of the popular flowering pot plants.

AFRICAN VIOLETS (*Saintpaulia*) Avoid plants whose leaves are curled under at the edges for this indicates that they have been exposed to cold conditions. The best time to buy these plants is in summer when the weather is warm.

AZALEAS These are offered round about Christmas time. Plants should have plenty of flower buds showing colour with a reasonable number of flowers open.

CHRYSANTHEMUMS The flowers of dwarf pot chrysanthemums should be well open when you buy, for tight buds may not open indoors. The flowers last for several weeks.

CYCLAMEN These popular winter-flowering pot plants should be well flowered, with plenty of flower buds yet to open. Avoid plants with brown-edged petals for this indicates that the flowers are almost over.

POINSETTIA This is a popular Christmas-flowering pot plant with, generally, scarlet petal-like bracts (the flowers are very small and found in the centre of these bracts). The flowers should be in the bud stage when you buy; if they have finished and have dropped off this is an indication that the bracts may not last for much longer.

THE RIGHT PLANTS FOR YOUR HOUSE

In most homes different rooms provide different conditions for plants. Some may be warm with a dry atmosphere, others may be warm with humid air, while other rooms may be cool or even unheated. It is a good idea, therefore, to choose plants suited to specific rooms. The following list will help you to choose plants for each room in the house. The conditions indicated for each room are, of course, as found in the average home and temperatures may vary slightly, so treat these lists as a general guide.

The Living Room

Temperature is usually around 21°C (70°F), but it may be lower at night. The air is usually dry, especially if central heating is installed.

Try the following plants: *Aphelandra* (zebra plant), *Begonia* (foliage types), *Beloperone* (shrimp plant), bromeliads, cacti, *Chlorophytum* (spider plant), *Cissus* (kangaroo vine), *Cordyline*, *Dieffenbachia* (dumb cane), *Dracaena*, *Ficus* (rubber plants and figs), *Heptapleurum* (parasol plant), *Impatiens* (busy lizzie), *Maranta* (prayer plant), *Monstera* (Swiss cheese plant), palms, *Philodendron*, *Schefflera* (umbrella plant), *Scindapsus* (devil's ivy), *Spathiphyllum*, *Syngonium* (arrowhead plant), *Tradescantia* and *Zebrina* (wandering Jew).

Dining Room and Bedrooms

These are generally cooler than the living room, with a temperature of around 16°C (60°F), the air is more humid and conditions generally more airy.

The following plants should do well: *Araucaria* (Norfolk Island pine), asparagus ferns, *Fatsia* (Japanese aralia), ferns of various kinds, *Ficus pumila* (creeping fig), *Grevillea* (silk oak), *Hedera* (ivy), *Saxifraga stolonifera* (mother of thousands), *Saintpaulia* (African violet).

Bathroom

This is often a warmish room with a temperature of around 16°C (60°F), but, above all, the air is very humid. Often there is not much direct sun. One could also use 'kitchen plants' in the bathroom.

Try the following: *Aglaonema* (Chinese evergreens), asparagus ferns, *Cyperus* (umbrella plants), *Dizygotheca* (false aralia), ferns, *Hypoestes* (polka dot plant), and *Rhoeo* (Moses in the cradle).

Left Many houseplants are enhanced if the light source is behind them. Here, palms create a dramatic effect in front of a window

Right Ferns, *Ficus benjamina* and asparagus ferns create a lush effect in this bathroom and are obviously growing well in the warm, steamy conditions

Below The kitchen is generally a warmish room with high humidity and good light — an ideal environment for a wide selection of houseplants

Kitchen

Generally this is another warmish room, with a temperature of around 16°C (60°F), although the temperature often fluctuates. Humidity is usually high and the light often very good. You could also use 'bathroom plants' in the kitchen.

The following can be recommended: bromeliads, *Episcia* (flame violet), *Fittonia* (mosaic plant), *Gynura* (velvet plant), *Maranta* (prayer plant), *Peperomia* (pepper elder), *Pilea* (aluminium plant), *Saintpaulia* (African violet), and short-term flowering pot plants in season.

Entry Hall, Staircase and Landing

These are generally considered the most difficult areas for plants. Due to the number of doors (including the front door) there could be draughts, and often there is poor natural light because there are few windows. The temperature may rise and fall — for instance, it may be around 16°C (60°F) during the day, falling at night to about 10°C (50°F). If central heating is used the air is bound to be dry. Tough plants are needed in these areas, particularly those able to take low temperatures.

The following are recommended: *Aspidistra* (cast-iron plant), *Campanula isophylla* (bellflower), *Chlorophytum* (spider plant), *Cissus* (kangaroo vine), *Clivia* (kaffir lily), hardier ferns like *Cyrtomium*, *Fatsia* (Japanese aralia), *Fatshedera*, *Hedera* (ivy), *Hydrangea*, *Sansevieria* (mother-in-law's tongue), and *Tolmiea* (pick-a-back plant).

USING PLANTS EFFECTIVELY

If you are artistically inclined you will be able to arrange your houseplants skilfully to create some very pleasing effects, but even if you are not, simply by following a few simple guidelines outlined here you should be able to arrange your plants in a tasteful and pleasing way. These are not hard and fast rules so do not feel you have to follow them to the letter.

Generally, foliage houseplants are used to form the 'framework' and give colour and interest throughout the year. Flowering houseplants can then be added in moderation, to give a splash of brighter colour here and there, perhaps among a group of mainly green foliage plants. Short-term flowering pot plants are useful to give colour at various seasons.

Arranging Plants in Groups

If possible try to avoid lining up several plants of the same height in a straight row, say on a windowsill. If this cannot be avoided then buy a windowsill trough and group your plants attractively in this. Try a tallish plant in the centre, grading down to shorter plants towards each end. Or perhaps tall plants at one end, grading down to shorter ones at the other.

If possible avoid having lots of small single plants dotted at random all over the place (but see Specimen Plants a little further on, page 14), as this usually creates a 'spotty' effect, which is neither particularly eye-catching nor pleasing.

The best effect is achieved when you group several plants together, perhaps to form a focal point in a room. Groups can also be used as room dividers, or for eye-catching displays in corners, alcoves or fireplaces. Groups can be created on the floor or on tables and other pieces of furniture.

Plants like to be grown together. They create their own micro-climate, the air is moist around them and generally they seem to grow much better. Do, however, make sure all the plants in any one group need the same conditions. It is no good growing tropical and virtually hardy plants together, for example. Some of the planted bowls that you see in shops, often around Christmas time, do not meet this requirement.

The majority of plants in a group can be foliage plants — with perhaps one or two pots of flowering plants to give bright colour. Avoid grouping too many coloured foliage plants together as the effect could be rather overpowering. Instead, go mainly for shades of green, with one or two subjects with coloured leaves.

You can achieve some marvellous contrasts in foliage shape and texture: for instance, try grouping plants with sword-like leaves with some which have bold hand- or heart-shaped foliage; and shiny-leaved plants with some which have felted or woolly leaves.

If the group is free-standing make sure it looks attractive from all angles. Tall plants can be placed in the middle, grading down to shorter and trailing plants towards the edges in what is roughly a pyramid shape. If the group is being created against a wall or some

Above Groups of plants can be arranged in corners of rooms provided there is sufficient light. This group illustrates good foliage contrast, which is achieved with a dwarf palm, weeping fig, grape ivy, ordinary ivies, dracaena and prayer plant or maranta

Above One way of arranging plants in a trough is to have tall plants at one end (a palm is used here), grading to shorter and trailing plants at the other (the trailers here are ivies). Other plants used in this attractive group include an azalea, wandering Jew and prayer plant

Right Some plants are better used as single specimens to create a room feature, particularly very large ones with distinctive foliage, such as palms of various kinds

other background, then aim for a triangular shape — tall plants in the centre, grading down to smaller ones towards the ends, and perhaps trailing kinds at the front.

An interesting effect can also be achieved by using plants of the same family in groups, instead of mixed plants. For example, groups of cacti or begonias can make a striking focal (and talking) point.

Single Specimens

Though you should avoid too many single plants dotted about haphazardly, as mentioned earlier, single plants can be used effectively, provided they are chosen with care, for they should have some feature which warrants them being grown in isolation — such as large bold foliage. Plants which look particularly good alone — and are ideal for creating a focal point in a room — include palms, *Monstera* (Swiss cheese plant), *Ficus* (rubber plants and figs), some of the large-leaved philodendrons, and plants with sword-like leaves such as *Yucca* and *Sansevieria* (mother-in-law's tongue).

Very large plants are best seen from a distance and therefore are most suitable for larger rooms. Other plants are best seen from above, particularly the bromeliads, although these also make good specimen plants. But some of the smaller plants should be viewed at close quarters, like *Calathea* and *Maranta* (prayer plant) to appreciate their beautiful leaf markings. These should make good specimen plants on a table.

BACKGROUNDS

It is safe to say that most houseplants are best displayed against a plain background rather than a heavily patterned one, for strong colours and patterns can detract from the beauty of plants. Indeed, many foliage plants with coloured leaves, and also flowers, can merge into heavily patterned wallpaper or curtains and hardly be noticed.

So, wherever possible, try to arrange your plants against plain walls. White or pastel-coloured tiles make a good background, as do cork tiles and hessian wallcoverings. Mirror tiles, or even large mirrors, can be an especially effective background, for they reflect light and also give the impression of twice as many plants, and therefore add depth to the group. Most natural materials make good backgrounds, like stone fireplaces and all kinds of wood.

Thin-leaved plants, like caladiums and some of the begonias, look particularly attractive when placed against windows so that the light shines through the leaves. This brings out colours otherwise unnoticed.

You must not forget the usefulness of climbing and trailing plants. Climbers can be trained up room dividers, used for lining archways and alcoves, for 'framing' windows or even for hiding ugly exposed pipework. They will also make single specimens to create focal points in a room.

Trailing plants can be used to soften the edges of groups, or for cascading over windowsills, tables, sideboards and so on. They also look attractive in hanging containers.

If there is an unsightly view from a window which you would rather like to hide, then consider putting up shelves in the window recess, across the width of the window and about 30cm (12in) apart. An assortment of plants can then be grouped on these, including some trailing kinds.

Decorative Containers

Flower pots are not particularly attractive, especially the plastic ones which are now in widespread use, and it is an advantage to hide them. To do this you can use ornamental pot holders which come in a wide range of materials such as china, pottery, plastic, wickerwork, brass and copper. Many garden centres carry a large assortment. Generally,

Below Some of the climbing houseplants, such as the Swiss cheese plant, are excellent for training on walls and around windows. It is recommended that the majority of houseplants used are foliage kinds, with a few flowering plants (such as Busy Lizzie, shown here) to provide spots of colour

Right Mirrors make a good background for plants – here an asparagus fern is beautifully reflected in this mirror-topped table

plain colours are better than heavy patterns, so that the pot holder does not detract from the beauty of the plant. Sometimes household items can be used — copper cooking pots or brass coal scuttles, for example. Buy a pot holder larger than the pot, so that the space between holder and pot can be filled with peat. By keeping the peat moist a desirable humid atmosphere can be maintained around the plant. If you have a porous pot holder, such as wickerwork, then first place a drip tray of suitable size in the bottom to catch surplus water.

Groups of plants can be arranged in large 'planters', which are basically ornamental boxes in various materials, like wood or plastic. Generally these are stood on the floor. Do not plant directly in the box, for roots will become entangled and then it will be difficult to remove and re-arrange the plants at a later date. Instead, keep the plants in their pots but plunge them up to their rims in peat or a horticultural aggregate. The peat or aggregate should be kept moist to create humidity.

It is also possible to buy deep window-sill troughs and these can also be filled with peat or aggregate and the pots plunged to their rims.

If the time you can spare for looking after houseplants is limited, you should consider the advantages of using self-watering pots. In these the plant is put into one of the usual compost mixes, which will then take up water as necessary from a built-in reservoir in the bottom of the pot. These pots are ornamental, quite expensive but useful if you have to leave plants for long periods, for the water in the special reservoir will last a long time.

There are all sorts of 'plant stands' available, in wrought iron, wood and cane, and some very pleasing displays can be created in them. There is an interesting range of hanging containers, too, but more about these in Chapter Five, see page 81.

TOOLS AND EQUIPMENT

POTS You will need pots of various sizes for potting on plants. Plastic pots are mainly used. Bear in mind these are not porous and compost takes longer to dry out, so be careful when watering them. Clay or terra-cotta pots are still available, and are porous, so compost dries out more quickly. They are ideal for plants which like well-drained, dryish conditions, like cacti and succulents. Half pots, in plastic or clay, are half the depth of normal flower pots and are ideal for low-growing and trailing plants.

You can obtain drip trays to fit most sizes of pot. Or gravel trays can be used for a collection of plants. These are shallow trays filled with horticultural aggregate or peat, which is kept moist to create humidity.

COMPOSTS Unless you are experienced, it is best to buy proprietary potting composts rather than to mix your own. You have a choice of soil-based (the John Innes composts), or soilless (consisting of peat, or peat and sand). The former are easier for the beginner to manage as there is little risk of making them too wet, for drainage is very good. They dry out quicker than peat-based composts. The John Innes composts are suitable for most houseplants, but on the other hand, soilless composts are now very widely used.

Becoming very popular, and especially recommended for beginners, are the multi-purpose composts which can be used for potting, seed sowing and for rooting cuttings. There are also available proprietary composts specifically for houseplants.

If you are potting lime-hating plants, such as azaleas, then use a lime-free or

'ericaceous compost'. For cacti, special cactus compost is available, while for spring bulbs, use a proprietary 'bulb fibre'. All of these are available from most good garden centres.

Odds and Ends

There are various other miscellaneous items you will need for houseplant care, including: a small watering can with a long spout; a hand sprayer; a sharp knife or secateurs; a soft brush for dusting off hairy-leaved plants and cacti; bamboo canes and short split canes for supporting plants, plus soft string; proprietary 'leaf-shine'; and houseplant fertilizer (available in liquid or tablet form).

'Luxury' items, which are useful to have but by no means essential, include a soil-moisture meter (indicates whether or not a plant needs watering); a maximum/minimum thermometer; and a humidity meter (indicates the moisture content of the atmosphere).

Above Plants in troughs can be arranged in a pyramid shape. The taller plants here are variegated ivy and mother-in-law's tongue. The lower growers include syngonium or goose foot, ivies and a polka dot plant with pink leaves

Left A variegated ivy and a philodendron provide height in this trough, while the lower-growing foliage plants make an attractive foil to the dwarf pot chrysanthemum

CHAPTER TWO

HOW PLANTS WORK

Opposite The Kaffir lily, or *Clivia miniata*, is used as ground cover in warmer climates, but makes an excellent flowering pot plant in the home, needing a moderately heated room and plenty of direct light, plus some sun

VARIOUS TYPES OF plant are grown as houseplants, and most of them are evergreen rather than deciduous — that is, their leaves persist throughout the year as opposed to falling in the autumn.

Some houseplants, such as crotons and cordylines, are shrubs and others are trees (at least in the wild, but not when pot grown). Typical examples are rubber plants and many of the palms. These all have tough woody stems. Then there are climbers, like cissus, often again with woody stems.

Another group of plants are the herbaceous perennials, such as maranta, peperomia and the bromeliads. The stems of these plants are soft and green, as opposed to being hard and woody. Perennial plants, like shrubs, trees and climbers, live for many years, their life span depending on the species.

Another group of plants which includes some houseplants among its members is that which comprises the bulbs, corms

and tubers — plants with swollen underground organs. An example is the cyclamen, which produces a tuber. These also live for a number of years, but their foliage generally dies down at some period during the year and the plants take a rest.

Lastly there are herbaceous and annual plants that are discarded after flowering — these are flowering pot plants like primulas, cinerarias and calceolarias. Some (the herbaceous kinds) can be kept but do not make much of a show the following year. The true annuals die naturally after they have flowered and set seeds.

It is useful to know how plants 'work', and to have an understanding of their natural habitats, in order to provide the right conditions for them.

In any one room, plants from very different natural habitats are often grown together: for instance, from tropical rain forests where it is hot and humid; deserts, where conditions are hot and dry; and from temperate forests, where conditions may be cool and moist, or warm and dryish. In order to keep them growing well it will be necessary to provide the right conditions for all these different types of plant.

A very large number of our houseplants originate from the tropics or subtropics in various parts of the world: South and Central America and the West Indies, Tropical Africa, South Africa, Madagascar, India, South-East Asia (includes Malaysia), and Australia and the Pacific Islands.

Others, fewer in number, come from temperate areas like Central and Eastern Asia (China and Japan), Europe, North America and New Zealand.

In general, the temperature and light

Right The purple-leaved form of *Cordyline australis* makes an attractive tree in warm climates. It is also a dramatic specimen plant in a cool room

Above Cacti are natives of arid places and will thrive in a centrally heated room with a dry atmosphere, provided the light is good and they receive some sunshine. Many are very free flowering, contrary to popular belief

which originate from South Africa, like clivia and vallota, are also able to store water in these swollen underground organs, to tide them over their dormant period during long, often exceedingly hot, summers. Generally the bulbs, corms and tubers are easy to grow in the home.

LIGHT AND SHADE

Light is essential to plants in order that they can manufacture foods — sugars and starches. The green pigment in the leaves (or in the stems of leafless plants like many cacti) is known as chlorophyll. It absorbs energy from sunlight and uses this energy to combine carbon dioxide and water into glucose, which is a simple sugar. During this process oxygen is given off through the leaves. The correct name for this process is photosynthesis.

The plant uses this simple sugar to form new cells or 'tissue'; or it may change it into starch, which is stored for use in the future.

Various complex chemical changes take place within the plant to turn the simple sugar into all the other substances which are found in plants — oil, for example.

If there is insufficient light for a plant, the amount of chlorophyll will be reduced and consequently photosynthesis will be reduced. This results in weak or poor growth.

Optimum light varies from one type of plant to another: some plants, such as those from tropical forests, have adapted to low light levels; others, such as the desert cacti, to high levels of light. The former can be grown in shade, the latter need plenty of sun.

At night (during darkness) photosynthesis stops and another process, called respiration, takes over. The plant uses oxygen to turn sugar into energy, which it needs to grow. There is a waste product of respiration — carbon dioxide — and this escapes through the leaves. In fact, all gaseous exchange is through the leaves. The leaves contain, mainly on their undersides, pores or stomata to facilitate this.

A plant grows towards a light source, so if light is coming from all directions, including above, then the plant grows in a well-balanced way. Generally this can only be obtained in a greenhouse. Indoors, light generally comes from one side, through a window, and so a plant

intensity in the average room suit tropical rain-forest plants, but usually there is not enough humidity and so this must be provided artificially. Some are easily grown while others are more difficult. Many of the plants which originate from tropical rain forests grow on or near the forest floor, where light intensity is very low, and so they have evolved very large leaves to ensure they are able to absorb sufficient energy from what sunlight there is. It is also interesting to note that the leaves of these forest dwellers are able to shed water very quickly, for a tremendous amount of rain falls throughout the year. Leaves are often smooth and shiny, and have an elongated tip to shed the water. Consequently these plants are often highly decorative, and that is why they are popular for use in the home.

Plants from very dry warm areas are generally easy to grow if given good light, say a sunny windowsill. They can generally survive a wide range of temperatures and like a dry atmosphere. Cacti and succulents are good examples. These plants often lack leaves, and have swollen stems to store water to tide them over dry periods. The stems carry out the usual leaf functions.

Bulbs, corms and tubers, many of

Water

Oxygen

Sunlight

Sugar

Carbon
dioxide

Respiration alone
occurs in the hours of
darkness

Photosynthesis and
respiration take place
in daylight

will grow in that direction. If the plant is not turned regularly, so that all parts receive light, it will gradually bend over as it grows toward the light.

If the light source is far away from a plant the intensity will be very low. Unless the plant is used to very poor light it will become 'drawn' and spindly (etiolated).

WATER AND AIR

Water evaporates from the leaves and this process is known as transpiration. The water vapour escapes through the pores or stomata. Transpiration is speeded up by dry air, high temperatures, wind and draughts. This process draws water up from the soil or compost through the roots.

Many plants have leaves and stems coated with waxy substances which slow the rate of transpiration, or water loss. Examples, again, are many cacti and succulents.

During hot weather transpiration can exceed water uptake, so plants may wilt or flag, and if this condition persists they could eventually die. Quite simply, there is not enough water in the plants.

Water loss through the leaves is made up by applying water to the compost or soil. The rate of transpiration can be reduced by providing a humid or moisture-laden atmosphere around the plants — by spraying the leaves with water, or standing the plants on or in a moisture-holding material like peat or horticultural aggregate, which is kept moist.

Generally speaking, plants with waxy, hairy or tough leathery leaves lose water less rapidly than thin-leaved plants and can be grown in a dry atmosphere, whereas the thin-leaved kinds need moist air.

In order to apply the right amount of water and humidity it is necessary to have some idea of the plant's natural habitat. Plants are adapted to natural rainfall and this must be borne in mind when watering.

For instance, many desert plants like cacti are used to long periods without rain, followed by a short rainy season, so keep them dry in autumn and winter and water them during spring and summer.

Other plants, like those from tropical rain forests, are used to rain throughout the year. There is a lot of rain in summer (the wet season) and less in winter (the

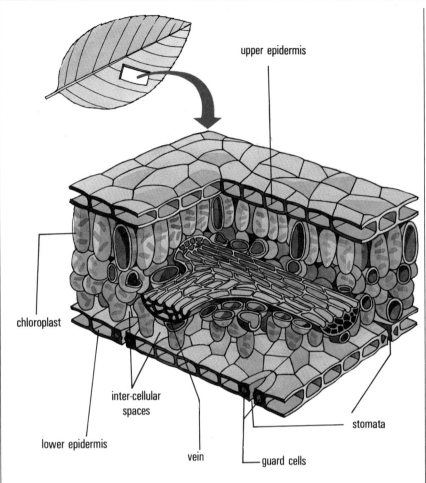

upper epidermis

chloroplast

inter-cellular
spaces

lower epidermis

vein

guard cells

stomata

Above A section of a leaf showing the pores or stomata, through which gaseous exchange occurs and water vapour is given off. Stomata are generally on the undersides of the leaves

so-called dry season, even though it may rain every day). These plants should be watered accordingly.

TEMPERATURE

The optimum temperature to provide depends, yet again, on the plant's natural habitat and seasonal needs. In the tropics the temperature is fairly constant all the year round. It is an interesting fact, however, that many tropical plants have been found to survive in lower temperatures than in their natural habitats. For example, bromeliads will tolerate quite low winter temperatures.

You should try to avoid sudden changes in temperature, though. A sudden drop or rise can result in leaf drop, wilting and even death.

The most difficult environment for plants is the room which is heated sporadically: for example, heated in the evenings only. Gradual variations in temperature do not usually cause any problems: for example, a decrease from 16°C

(60°F) to 10°C (50°F), caused by turning down the central heating at night. In natural habitats temperatures often do drop at night — it can be quite chilly in a tropical rain forest during the hours of darkness. However, if you allow the temperature to fall below 10°C (50°F), then most tropical plants start to suffer.

The type of heating used may affect plants — for instance, some, like begonias, cannot abide gas heating.

Contrary to widely held belief, excessive heat can result in physical damage and even death. Perhaps too high a temperature is not likely indoors, but it certainly can occur in a greenhouse or conservatory, especially if, during a very hot spell, all the ventilators are closed and there is no shading. Once the temperature goes above 38°C (100°F) some plants start to become troubled.

The temperature should be considered in conjunction with other factors — light, water and humidity. Generally speaking, the higher the temperature the more light, humidity and water needed. There is a good example — which many gardeners may have discovered: if seedlings are raised early in the year in a high temperature, when the natural light level is low, they will become very drawn and spindly. In this situation artificial lighting should be provided to ensure sturdy growth.

The lower the temperature, the less water and humidity needed, and light levels need not be so high.

FOOD

Plants can live on the simple sugar (glucose) plus water, but for really healthy balanced growth they need minerals (also known as nutrients). These are obtained from the soil or compost, usually from fertilizers which are included in the potting or seed composts, and which are applied at later stages, too.

These nutrients are dissolved in water and the plant absorbs this solution through fine root hairs on the tips of the main roots.

The water and dissolved nutrients are carried all through the plant via an elaborate 'plumbing system' known as the xylem (a system of tubes). This solution is called the sap. Some of the tubes are clearly visible — the 'veins' in leaves, for example.

There is another tube system, too, called the phloem. This transports simple sugar (glucose), which is made in the leaves, to all the other parts of the plant.

Soil or compost, then, is used not only for supporting the plant and anchoring the roots, but also for supplying water and foods.

However, soil or compost is not always used: there is a system of growing known as hydroponics, where plants are grown in a nutrient solution. In indoor systems, the plant is anchored in an inert, horticultural aggregate.

Some plants can be grown without their roots in compost or nutrient solution — these are the air plants or epiphytic tillandsias, in the bromeliad family. Indeed, these plants make very little root, as they absorb sufficient moisture and nutrients through their leaves. Needless to say, they come from tropical rain forests where there is plenty of atmospheric moisture, and where they grow on the forest trees. Indoors, they can be attached to a piece of wood, such as driftwood, and moisture supplied simply by spraying the leaves with plain water. Occasionally a little liquid fertilizer can be added, to ensure the plants have sufficient nutrients. Further details on cultivation of these interesting plants can be found in Chapter Five, page 85.

Compost Mixes

Compost must also contain air (unless the plant is an aquatic and specially adapted to absorb oxygen from the surrounding water). In a free-draining compost there are many small pockets of air. If the compost becomes waterlogged these air spaces become filled with water, the air being pushed out. When the compost is in this condition the roots of the plant cannot breathe and so the plant drowns. Therefore, do make sure that you do not keep the compost saturated with water. This can happen if the pot stands in a drip tray which is filled with surplus water, and you carry on watering from above.

Lack of air in a compost also results in the death of beneficial soil organisms (bacteria) and so the result is a lifeless, sour rooting medium.

Not all water in soil or compost is available to the plant. Soil holds water in tension. The lower the water content the greater the tension, so the drier the soil or compost becomes the more difficult it is for the plant to absorb the remaining water. The plant does not have this problem when the compost is moist.

To summarize, it is sensible to grow your houseplants in a good compost, well aerated and drained and containing fertilizer. Do not use garden soil, as this does not have the correct texture or quantity of foods for houseplants, even though garden plants may grow well in it.

It is important to apply more fertilizer to the compost later on, after the plants have become established in their pots. This must be done before the fertilizer in the compost runs out. When this happens the plants quickly take on a starved appearance and growth slows down.

One cannot go wrong by growing houseplants in the proprietary potting composts, like the John Innes range. J.I. potting compost No. 1 is used mainly for potting off rooted cuttings and seedlings (in other words, young plants). J.I. No. 2, which contains twice as much fertilizer, is used for potting on most plants, while J.I. No. 3, containing three times as much fertilizer, is used for plants in large pots, and for large or very vigorous growers. One can also use the soilless or peat-based equivalents of John Innes.

While cuttings can be rooted in a compost which contains no plant foods (e.g. a mixture of peat and sand), as soon as they have rooted they must be potted into a potting compost so that foods are available. If you cannot do this at the optimum time, then do at least feed the rooted cuttings with a liquid fertilizer once a week until such time as they are potted off.

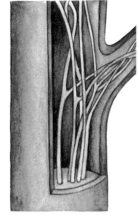

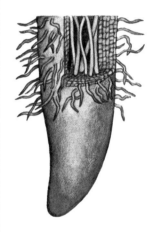

Above A diagram of the 'plumbing system', which carries water and dissolved nutrients through the plant. *Below* Root hairs at the tip of a main root

Below A truly spectacular bromeliad – *Neoregelia carolinae tricolor*. The centre is kept filled with fresh water

CHAPTER THREE

CULTIVATION AND CARE

Opposite A contrast in foliage shape and colour, provided by crotons, dumb cane, ivies and a variegated dracaena

Below When and how to water houseplants probably causes more problems for the newcomer than any other aspect of care

HOUSEPLANTS NEED regular care and attention: watering, feeding, cleaning, potting, and so on. It is advisable to make sure you have time for all of this so that your plants remain attractive and healthy.

There is, of course, a great temptation among gardeners to fill their homes with plants but in doing so it is important to remember that maintenance takes up a great deal of time. There are few worse sights than a house full of neglected, badly grown plants. So the number of plants that you grow should be restricted to that which you can look after properly. The practical advice in this chapter will ensure your plants thrive.

WATERING

Watering causes many houseplant owners more problems than perhaps any other aspect of cultivation. There is a great temptation to over-water plants rather than under-water and this is particularly harmful.

As a general rule, plants need more water in the growing season, in warm or hot conditions, when they are in a dry atmosphere and when they are in bud or flower. Again, in general, watering is increased when plants start into growth in mid-spring and is decreased in early autumn as growth slows down.

WHEN TO WATER Many people find it difficult to decide how often to water plants and, very wrongly, may apply a 'splash' of water daily. This is a case of killing plants with kindness.

If the pot is completely filled with roots, the plant will need watering more frequently than one which has not completely permeated the compost with roots. Newly potted plants therefore need less frequent watering than well-established specimens.

Bear in mind, too, that peat composts dry out more slowly than the soil-based kinds; the latter will need checking more frequently. However, once peat-based composts dry right out they are more difficult to moisten again.

Wilting can indicate water shortage but ideally one should not allow this to happen, for lack of water can result in

Above An African violet suffering from overwatering. This plant is best watered from below. *Top right* The leaves and stems of this primula are collapsing due to lack of moisture at the roots. *Right* When compost is excessively dry stand the pot up to its rim in water and remove when air bubbles cease to rise to the surface

Above A soil-moisture meter is a sure means of determining whether or not a plant needs watering. When the probe is pushed into the compost the calibrated dial will indicate 'wet', 'moist' or 'dry'

bud and flower drop. With excessive watering the symptoms are similar — leaves wilt, turn yellow and fall, and flower buds or flowers may drop. Do not allow pots to stand in water for this can saturate the compost. Tip surplus water out of drip trays after watering.

If you are growing plants in clay flower pots, it is easy to test for the moisture content of the compost. The pot can be tapped with a home-made 'hammer' — a cotton reel on the end of a cane. If this results in a ringing sound then the compost is dry. If it is a dull thud then the compost is moist.

You can also tell whether or not water is required by the weight of the pot, especially if it is a plastic pot or one containing peat-based compost. The pot will be light in weight if the compost is dry and heavier if moist.

Another, and very reliable, way of telling whether or not a plant needs watering is to feel the surface of the compost with a finger. Prod it to a depth of about 2.5cm (1in) and if it feels dry to this depth then apply water.

Another method of testing for water requirements is to use one of the proprietary soil-moisture meters. These

have a probe which is pushed into the compost, and a calibrated dial indicates 'wet', 'moist' and 'dry'.

METHODS OF WATERING When you have decided that water is needed, give a thorough soaking by filling the pot to the rim so that the full depth of compost is moistened. A quick 'splash' will only penetrate the surface, leaving the rest of the compost dry. After a 'good' watering leave the plant well alone until the compost is starting to become dry again.

If the compost has been allowed to become very dry (either by neglect or for the purpose of resting plants, like cacti) normal watering with a watering can from above will not be effective for moistening the complete volume of compost. This is certainly the case with very dry peat composts. Instead, use the technique of standing the pot up to its rim in water and leave it there until air bubbles have stopped rising from the compost to the surface of the water. Then remove the pot and let it drain.

Certain plants require different methods of watering. Epiphytic (tree-dwelling) plants, which are being grown on pieces of wood, particularly many of the bromeliads or air plants, are simply sprayed daily with water, which is taken in through the leaves and stems. If you grow the bromeliads whose leaves form a 'vase', like urn plants (*Aechmea*) then, apart from watering the compost, the 'vase' should be kept filled with water. This should not be allowed to become stagnant, so every three or four weeks empty it out and refill with fresh water. In the interim period check regularly and top up if necessary. With cacti and succulents the compost should be allowed to become almost dry between waterings.

You should avoid wetting the leaves of some plants when watering. Especially vulnerable kinds include African violets (*Saintpaulia*), gloxinias and other plants with velvety, hairy or woolly leaves. Also avoid water collecting on top of cyclamen tubers. All of these plants may rot if not watered carefully. If watering from above is a problem, then stand the pots up to their rims in water as explained earlier.

The best time to water houseplants is in the morning, because the temperature is rising and the need for water is greater. Plants left damp overnight, often when the temperature drops, are more prone to diseases like grey mould.

There is no doubt that 'soft' water is

best for watering houseplants (that is, water free from lime or chalk). It is essential for lime-hating plants, such as azaleas and heathers, and very desirable for bromeliads.

Your tap water may be soft, but if you live in a hard-water area try, if possible, to collect rainwater for your houseplants. Or use distilled water for the 'touchy' subjects like azaleas. The majority of houseplants accept hard water, though, so do not worry too much about water quality.

Holiday Care

These days it is easy to ensure your houseplants have sufficient moisture while you are on holiday, by setting up a simple capillary watering system on the draining board. Spread a sheet of capillary matting (available from garden centres) on the draining board and allow one end to go well down into the sink, which should be partly filled with water. Stand the plants on the matting. Water travels up from the sink to keep the matting moist and plants take up moisture as they need it. This only works with plastic pots, the bases of which should be in really close contact with the matting. If you cannot use this method consider buying one of the clear polythene 'tents' specially designed to keep houseplants in good condition while you are away. The plants are completely enclosed and therefore the compost does not dry out quickly.

Providing Humidity

To provide plants with a humid or moist atmosphere, either plunge the pots to their rims in peat or horticultural aggregate, in a large container, or stand the pots on trays of gravel. Keep these materials moist but do not allow plants to stand in water. An alternative method of providing humidity is to spray plants daily or twice daily with plain water (but not plants with woolly, hairy or velvety leaves). There is no need to saturate the leaves so that water drips all over the floor — a light spraying with a fine sprayer is all that is necessary. Do not spray plants that are standing in hot sunshine, however, for the water droplets act as mini magnifying glasses and this results in brown scorch marks on the leaves.

FEEDING

As with watering, there is a tendency to over-feed houseplants — to apply too much fertilizer in one go, or to apply it too often.

The main period for applying fertilizer is between mid-spring and early autumn when most plants are in active growth. Do not feed in autumn or winter when growth has slowed down or stopped, although flowering pot plants can be fed until the time they come into bloom. Dormant or resting plants should not be fed, irrespective of the time of the year.

Do not apply fertilizer to compost if it is very dry. Water it well first and allow the plants to become fully charged with water.

Newly potted plants should not be fed, for there will be sufficient fertilizer in the compost. Leave them for approximately six to eight weeks, until the plants are established and have sent out new roots.

How often should houseplants be fed? For the majority, every two weeks in the growing season is sufficient. However, very vigorous plants, or any which are pot-bound, can, with advantage, be fed weekly.

Above Plants can be kept moist while you are on holiday by means of capillary wicks, with the ends placed in a bowl of water. Wicks can be made from strips of capillary matting

Left Do not feed houseplants in the autumn or winter when growth has slowed down or stopped
Below left When new growth is apparent, such as a leaf unfurling, plants can be fed at regular intervals
Below Flowering plants can be fed up until the time they come into bloom

Plants in peat-based compost may need feeding more frequently than those in soil-based composts for the former cannot hold on to plant foods as well as the latter.

There are proprietary fertilizers available which have been specially formulated for houseplants, both flowering and foliage kinds, containing the right amounts of the major nutrients (nitrogen, phosphorus and potash), as well as minor but important foods. There is even a special fertilizer for African violets (*Saintpaulia*).

Most fertilizers for houseplants are concentrated liquids (often based on seaweed) which have to be diluted with water. Others, usually general-purpose fertilizers, are powders which have to be dissolved in water. Then there are fertilizer tablets specially for house- and other potted plants, which are pushed into the compost where they will release their nutrients over several weeks.

Foliar fertilizers are applied as a spray to the leaves and are rapidly absorbed by plants. These give a quick boost to growth and are especially useful for feeding epiphytic plants which are being grown on wood, and for climbers, including those being grown up moss poles. Foliar feeds can also be given to plants which are suffering from shortage of food, but, in these cases, fertilizer must also be applied to the compost.

Always follow the manufacturers' instructions on the use of fertilizers, because an overdose can seriously harm plants.

GENERAL CARE

Remove dead, dying and yellowing leaves, and dead flowers, as this not only discourages pests and diseases but also improves the appearance of plants.

Regularly sponge off leaves with tepid water to keep them free from dust and dirt, because a layer of grime impairs the functioning of the leaves. Plants with glossy foliage can be treated with one of the proprietary leaf-shine materials after cleaning, to give a high gloss, although some people may consider this looks a bit unnatural. Do not use it on very soft young leaves or it may damage them.

Do not sponge off plants with woolly, hairy or velvety leaves but instead dust them with a soft brush. This also applies to cacti.

A green growth often develops on the surface of compost (especially peat composts) and, although not harmful to plants, it is unsightly. This is algae, a primitive form of plant life. It is easily removed by scraping it off with an old knife. If necessary, top up with fresh compost. Regular stirring of the compost surface often helps to prevent algae developing.

Some plants may need pinching out when young to encourage bushy growth and this certainly applies to some of the trailing kinds such as wandering Jew (*Tradescantia* and *Zebrina*). Cut out the tips of shoots before they become too long. Young climbers generally benefit from this treatment, too.

Plants which become bare at the base, such as many of the climbers and also dumb cane (*Dieffenbachia*) and rubber plants (*Ficus*), can be cut back hard to leave 15cm (6in). They will then produce new shoots from the base. Shoots which have been removed can be used as cuttings, if you want more plants.

Some plants will need tying in regularly to supports, to keep them neat and tidy, and, of course, this applies especially to climbers. Use soft green garden string, and do not tie in tightly (allow room for the stems to thicken). Use a figure-of-eight loop around the stem and cane or other support.

Provide canes or other supports at the time of potting, but no higher than the

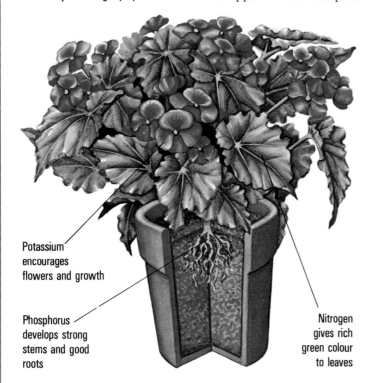

Below The three plant foods essential for healthy growth are nitrogen, phosphorus and potash. These are contained in proprietary houseplant fertilisers in just the right proportions

Potassium encourages flowers and growth

Phosphorus develops strong stems and good roots

Nitrogen gives rich green colour to leaves

plant. Canes, etc., should reach the bottom of the pot. As the plant grows, replace with longer canes or supports, inserting them into the same hole to avoid root damage.

For weak-stemmed or spreading plants, twiggy sticks make good supports, inserted while the plants are small. As the plants grow, they will hide the sticks.

There are various proprietary wire plant supports on the market, including hoops for climbers and pot trellis in various designs.

POTTING

There are several methods of potting involved in the care of houseplants. Initially, there is potting-off, in which seedlings and newly rooted cuttings are transferred from the seed or cutting compost to their first pots. Generally 7.5-cm (3-in) pots are large enough, and not too rich a compost — use John Innes potting compost No. 1 or one of the various kinds of soilless equivalent.

First place a layer of compost in the bottom of the pot and firm it moderately. Carefully lift the cutting or seedling and hold it so that it is central in the pot and the roots are dangling straight down. Fill the pot to the top with compost and give it a tap on the bench to ensure the compost settles down. Firm all round

with your fingers and add more compost to take the level to within 12mm (½in) of the pot rim. Water well to settle the compost around the seedling or cutting.

Potting-on involves moving a plant to a larger pot before it becomes pot-bound. For most, this means using the next size of pot. It is not a good idea to let houseplants become too large for their pots, for the root restriction slows down growth.

How do you know when a plant needs potting-on? The obvious indication is when roots start growing out of the drainage holes. To check further the state of the roots, invert the pot, tap the rim on the edge of a table or bench, and slide out the rootball. If there is a mass of roots, with little compost visible, then pot-on. If there is a lot of compost visible, with only a few roots showing through, then the plant does not need moving.

Do not use too large a pot for potting-on — there should be no more than about 2.5cm (1in) of space between the rootball and the sides of the new pot. However, for quick growers, like some of the temporary flowering pot plants, you generally move them on to pots which are two sizes larger — e.g. from 9cm (3½in) to 12.5cm (5in). A richer compost is used for potting-on — John Innes potting compost No. 2 or soilless equivalent. For very large or vigorous plants, John Innes potting compost No. 3 is often used.

Potting-on is generally carried out in

Left Not all rubber plants have plain green leaves: there are several varieties available which are variegated in cream and green. The leaves should be cleaned regularly to maintain the attractive appearance

Right Most plants should be potted on to larger-size pots before the compost becomes tightly packed with roots (when the plant is said to be pot-bound).

When potting-on to a larger pot, trickle compost between the rootball and the sides of the pot, working it well down with your fingers.

The compost should be firmed with the fingers, lightly for peat-based types, moderately for soil-based

mid-spring, but may also be needed during the growing season; particularly for young, short-term flowering pot plants, which must be kept growing steadily.

Always use clean pots, and for those over 15cm (6in) in diameter, it is recommended that drainage material is placed in the bottom. A layer of broken clay pots (crocks) is the usual drainage material. The compost should be moist — not wet or very dry.

Place a layer of compost in the bottom of the pot, firm it moderately, place the rootball in the centre and trickle compost around it. Tap the pot on the bench to get the compost well down, firm with the fingers, and add more compost to within 12–25mm (½–1in) of the pot rim, depending on size of pot. Water well in.

The technique of re-potting is sometimes used for mature plants when further increase in size is not required but the present pot is full of roots. The plant is returned to the same sized pot

after some of the old compost is replaced with new. The size of the rootball needs to be reduced, but new roots will be produced to replace those removed. Some of the old compost is teased away and roots pruned back with secateurs.

If you find that a plant is difficult to remove from its pot, slide a long-bladed knife all round between the rootball and the side of the pot, right down to the bottom. This will loosen the rootball and it should then slide out. To remove a plant from a very large pot — say 30cm (12in) and upwards—lay the plant on the floor, hold the stems and get someone else to tap the rim of the pot with a block of wood until it can be slid off. Ideally two people will also be needed for potting a large specimen.

PROPAGATION

Producing new houseplants is good fun and generally very easy. Many subjects can be rooted easily from cuttings, and a wide range of houseplants, flowering and foliage kinds, can be raised from seeds. Seeds can be obtained from garden centres or direct from well-known seedsmen.

To be sure of success it is well worth-while investing in a small electrically heated propagating case — perhaps one of the windowsill models — which cost only a few pence a week to run. These ensure a temperature of around 21°C (70°F) which is ideal for raising all kinds of seeds and cuttings. And the clear-plastic dome or cover ensures high humidity within — necessary for the successful rooting of many cuttings.

If you do not have a propagating case,

seeds can be germinated in a warm airing cupboard, but the seedlings, as soon as they appear, must be moved into good light — say a warm windowsill. Pots of cuttings can be completely enclosed in a clear polythene bag, supported with a few split canes, and placed on a windowsill in a warm room. The bag should be opened up several times a week, for an hour or so, to allow condensation to evaporate.

Seeds

As you will probably need only small quantities, seeds can be sown in a 9cm (3½in) pot, using John Innes seed compost or one of the soilless equivalents. Sow very thinly on a smooth level surface according to instructions on the packet. Very fine dust-like seeds should not be covered with compost, but larger ones should be covered with a layer equal to about twice their diameter. After sowing, moisten the compost — stand the pots almost up to their rims in water until the surface of the compost becomes damp. Some Cheshunt Compound could be added to the water, as this fungicide prevents damping-off disease (when the seedlings suddenly collapse and die).

When seedlings are large enough to handle easily, they are pricked out or potted-off into small pots. Very tiny or slow-growing seedlings, however, may need to be pricked out into a seed tray, to grow on, before potting-off. They are moved on before they become overcrowded in the tray.

Stem Cuttings

A very wide range of houseplants can be propagated from stem cuttings. These are prepared from soft side shoots, or from tips of shoots, generally as soon as young material is available, between mid-spring and late summer. It is best to use shoots which do not contain flower buds or flowers.

Select a sturdy young shoot and remove it with a sharp knife (this is essential, for clean, smooth, as opposed to ragged, cuts are necessary). To prepare the cutting, cut the stem at the base immediately below a leaf joint (node), where the leaves join the stem. Aim for a cutting about 5–7.5cm (2–3in) long. Do not remove the tip. Cut off the lower leaves, so that the lower third to half of

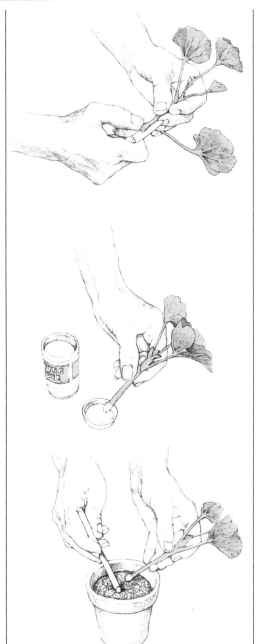

Left Many houseplants can be propagated from stem cuttings, prepared from young side shoots.

Rooting of cuttings is speeded up if the bases are dipped in a hormone rooting powder.

Most cuttings root best in a cutting compost, which is a mixture of equal parts peat and sand. Insert cuttings up to the lower leaves

the cutting is stripped of all foliage.

The lower 6mm (¼in) should be dipped in hormone rooting powder to encourage and speed up rooting. Do not dip the cutting in water first because this results in too much powder adhering to the base of the cutting.

Then insert the cuttings up to the level of the lower leaves in pots of cutting compost — a mixture of equal parts peat and coarse sand. Or use one of the multipurpose peat-based composts. Water in, and root in the conditions described earlier. Pot off when roots have formed — indicated by the tips of the cuttings starting into growth.

Stem Sections

This is a fascinating method of propagation from cuttings taken without leaves. It is used mainly for houseplants with large leaves because normal cuttings of these would take up too much space in the propagating case.

Examples of plants that can be propagated from stem sections include: Chinese evergreens (*Aglaonema*), cabbage palm (*Cordyline*), dumb cane (*Dieffenbachia*), *Dracaena*, Swiss cheese plant (*Monstera*), *Philodendron*, *Scindapsus* and goose foot (*Syngonium*). Do not allow the sap of dumb cane to come in contact with your face or mouth, for it results in severe pain and swelling in the mouth and eyes.

Select young stems which are still green, not hard and woody. Sections of leafless stem can be used if still green; otherwise cut off the leaves just above the dormant bud in the leaf axil.

Cut the stems into 5–7.5cm (2–3in) long sections with a sharp knife or secateurs. Make sure you keep them the right way up so that the cuttings are not inserted upside down. Each section must contain at least one, ideally several, nodes or leaf joints, from which new growth will be produced. The lower end of each section should be dipped into hormone rooting powder. Push the sections vertically into pots of cutting compost so that the tops are level with or just above the surface. Root in the conditions described earlier. New shoots appear well before rooting takes place so do not be in too much of a rush to pot-off.

Cuttings in Water

A novel way of rooting cuttings of some houseplants is in jars of water on a warm windowsill. Prepare as for stem cuttings and stand them in a jar, adding just sufficient water to cover the stripped stems. When roots are about 2.5cm (1in) long, remove from the water and pot-off into compost. Subjects which respond to this method include crotons (*Codiaeum*), flame nettle (*Coleus*), fuchsias, busy lizzie (*Impatiens*), oleander (*Nerium oleander*), and wandering Jew (*Tradescantia* and *Zebrina*). It is well worth trying the method with other plants, too.

Leaf Cuttings

Some houseplants can be propagated from leaves, these being prepared in various ways according to the subject.

With some plants, for example pepper elders (*Peperomia*) and African violets (*Saintpaulia*), whole leaves are used, complete with the leaf stalk.

Remove some leaves, complete with stalks, and dip the bases of the stalks in hormone rooting powder. Insert in pots of cutting compost up to the base of the leaf blade.

Gloxinias and Cape primroses (*Streptocarpus*) are also propagated from entire leaves, but because these are on the long side they are generally cut in half, and the lower half used as a cutting.

Some begonias, particularly *B. rex* and *B. masoniana*, can be propagated from entire leaves. Remove a leaf and cut off

Right Cuttings of some plants root readily in water, such as busy lizzie (*Impatiens*)

Far right African violets can be increased from leaf cuttings but they need a fairly high temperature to root and produce little plants

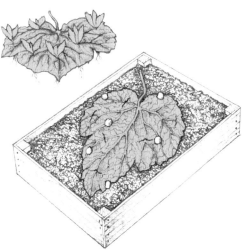

Division

A very easy way of increasing many houseplants is to split or divide them into a number of portions and to pot these off. The clump-forming plants can be treated in this way including the cast-iron plant (*Aspidistra*), bromeliads, many cacti and succulents, the spider plants (*Chlorophytum*), ferns, orchids, Mother-in-law's tongue (*Sansevieria*), and African violets (*Saintpaulia*).

Remove the plant from its pot, tease away as much compost as possible, and pull the plant apart or cut it apart with a sharp knife. Each portion must have a reasonable amount of top growth and roots. With many cacti it is often unnecessary to remove the plants from their pots — simply detach the offsets from around the main plant. With bromeliads, use the new growths from around the base of the old plant as divisions. The old plant dies after flowering, so divide the original plant once it starts to decline.

Divisions are then potted into suitable sized pots of potting compost. The normal time for dividing most houseplants is just as they are starting into growth in mid-spring.

Left An entire leaf of *Begonia rex* will produce several new plants. The veins on the underside are cut through before placing the leaf on the surface of the compost and weighting it down

the leaf stalk. Turn the leaf upside down and cut through the main veins in a number of places. Lay the leaf on the surface of cutting compost, in a tray, the right way up. The cut veins must touch the compost, so weigh down the leaf with small stones. Roots are produced where the veins have been cut through, and eventually new plants will appear.

Mother-in-law's tongue (*Sansevieria*) can be propagated from leaf cuttings, but if you have the cultivar with yellow-edged leaves, the new plants will not have this yellow edge. Cut a leaf into 5-cm (2-in) long sections, and make sure you keep them the right way up so they are not inserted upside down. Dip the bases in hormone rooting powder, and insert vertically to half their length in pots of cutting compost.

Some succulent plants can be increased from entire leaves. These include aloe, crassula, echeveria, and stonecrop (*Sedum*). Simply insert shallowly, and upright, in a pot of cutting compost.

The rubber plant (*Ficus elastica*) can be propagated from leaf-bud cuttings. Each cutting should consist of a 2.5-cm (1-in) length of young stem, at the top of which is a complete leaf with a growth bud in the leaf axil. Dip the base in hormone rooting powder, roll the leaf longitudinally and secure with an elastic band, so that it does not take up too much space in the propagating case. Insert the cutting in a 7.5-cm (3-in) pot of cutting compost, so that the top of the stem is only slightly above compost level. Support with a thin cane.

With all of these leaf or leaf-bud cuttings, young plants or new growth will eventually be produced at the base. Once they appear, lift and pot-off into small individual pots.

Left Large, established clump-forming plants, such as mother-in-law's tongue or sansevieria, can be increased by division in the spring

Above Bryophyllum daigremontianum produces little plants on the edges of the leaves. These can be removed and potted, when they will quickly form roots and start to grow

Plantlets

Some houseplants produce new plants on their leaves or stems and these can be used for propagation.

The succulent plants *Bryophyllum* (*Kalanchoe*) *daigremontianum* and *B. tubiflora* produce little plants on the leaves. Either remove these and pot them, or wait until they drop off and root into the compost — then lift them carefully and pot-off into small pots.

The pick-a-back plant (*Tolmiea menziesii*) produces plantlets at the base of the mature leaves. Peg down a leaf containing a plantlet onto the surface of the compost, in a small pot alongside the main plant. The plantlet will quickly root, and it can be cut away from the parent plant.

The spider plants (*Chlorophytum*) and the mother-of-thousands (*Saxifraga stolonifera*) produce young plants on the ends of long stems. These plantlets can be rooted in small pots of compost placed alongside the main plants. Simply peg down a plantlet onto the surface of the compost, using a piece of wire bent into the shape of a hairpin. Within a few weeks the plantlet will have rooted into the pot, and can be severed from the parent plant.

Right The plantlets of the spider plant or chlorophytum can be rooted in pots while still attached to the parent plant. Then they are cut away

Air Layering

This involves encouraging a portion of stem to produce roots while it is still attached to the parent plant. It is an easy way of securing new plants and also solves the problem of what to do with a large plant that reaches the ceiling. The top can be air layered and the rest of the plant cut back to a more manageable size.

Plants which respond to this method include crotons (*Codiaeum*), rubber plants and figs (*Ficus*), dracaena, and philodendrons.

About 30cm (12in) from the top of a stem make a cut half way through the stem, about 5cm (2in) in length and in an upward direction, to form a 'tongue'. Dust the cut with hormone rooting powder and then pack it with moist sphagnum moss to keep it open. The prepared part of the stem is then wrapped with moss which is held in place with a 'bandage' of clear polythene, sealed at the bottom and top with a few twists of waterproof tape.

Kept in a warm room, the stem should produce roots within a few weeks. As soon as white roots are seen through the polythene, unwrap it, cut off the rooted section just below the roots and pot-off into a suitable sized pot.

PESTS AND DISEASES

Even indoors plants cannot escape pests and diseases and, indeed, many of these multiply rapidly, and breed all the year round, in the favourable 'climate'. Not all plant ailments, though, are caused by pests and diseases — some are physiological disorders, and these are included under diseases in this chapter. Physio-

Far left The pick-a-back plant, or tolmiea, produces plantlets at the base of the leaves. These can be pegged down and rooted into pots while still attached to the parent plant

Left Several houseplants, such as the rubber plant, can be air layered. Near the top of the stem make a cut with a sharp knife to form a tongue and pack it with moist sphagnum moss to keep it open. Then this part of the stem is wrapped in moss which is held in place with a 'bandage' of clear polythene. Kept in a warm room, roots should start to show through the polythene within a matter of weeks

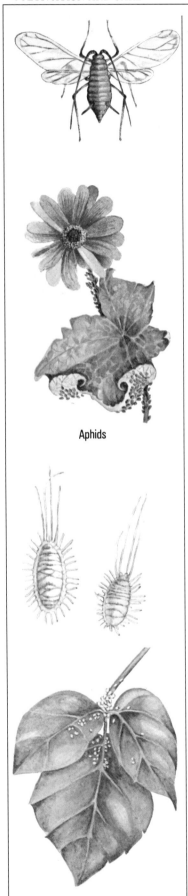

Aphids

Red spider mites

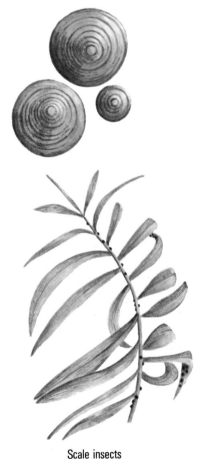

Scale insects

logical disorders are generally caused by incorrect cultivation, or growing a plant in an unsuitable environment.

If any pests and diseases are found on your plants, spray them thoroughly with a suitable insecticide or fungicide — preferably in a shed, garage or in the open. Do not spray plants exposed to strong sunlight, for fear of leaf scorch.

Pay particular attention to the undersides of the leaves when spraying, for often pests congregate there, and thoroughly wet the entire plant. You may need to repeat the application if the first does not completely clear up the trouble. Use pesticides strictly according to the manufacturer's instructions.

Pests

APHIDS These green or black plant bugs are found on shoot tips and young leaves, where they suck the sap and cause distortion. They quickly build up into large colonies. Spray with permethrin or dimethoate.

MEALY BUGS These are like large versions of aphids, but covered in white 'meal'. They cause the same damage as aphids and are particularly troublesome on woody plants and cacti and succulents. Spray with permethrin or malathion, or dab individually with a small paint brush dipped in methylated spirits.

RED SPIDER MITES Tiny red spider mites which are barely visible to the naked eye. They attack many plants, sucking the sap and causing fine, pale mottling on the leaves. A large colony produces fine webbing. Spray with permethrin or dimethoate.

SCALE INSECTS Immobile insects which look like scales on the stems and are brown or greyish in colour. Control is as described for mealy bugs.

VINE WEEVILS The white grubs with brown heads live in the soil and eat the roots, and the tubers of plants like cyclamen. The first sign of trouble is when the plant starts to wilt for no apparent reason. To eradicate, drench the compost with a solution of gama-HCH.

WHITEFLY These tiny pure white flies congregate on the undersides of the leaves and suck the sap. They produce

Mealy bugs

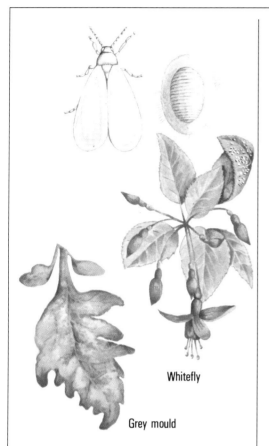

Whitefly

Grey mould

Leaf spots

Mildew

Virus

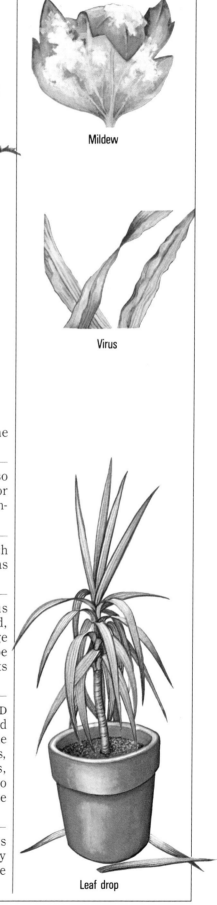

Leaf drop

sticky 'honeydew' on which sooty mould grows, giving the leaves an unattractive appearance. Spray with permethrin.

Diseases and Disorders

CHLOROSIS A disorder which affects lime-hating plants (like azaleas) when grown in compost containing lime or chalk. Use an acid compost. To cure symptoms (yellow leaves and stunted growth), drench the soil with a sequestered-iron formulation.

GREY MOULD This disease is also known as botrytis and can attack almost any plant. All parts are affected — leaves, stems, flowers. A grey mould develops, followed by rotting. Grey mould often infects wounds, and is also found on dead plant tissue, from where it can spread to healthy tissue. Remove affected parts of the plant. Spray regularly with benomyl until trouble clears up.

LEAF SPOTS Brown spots or scorch marks on leaves are caused by wetting the foliage when the plants are in full sun. Water droplets act as magnifying glasses and the leaves are literally burnt. If you

want to spray the leaves, make sure the plant is in the shade.

BROWN LEAF EDGES These can also be caused by wetting leaves in full sun, or by a dry atmosphere, draughts, and conditions which are too cold.

MILDEW White fungal patches which appear on leaves and shoot tips. Spray as soon as noticed with benomyl.

VIRUSES These cause various symptoms. Leaves may become mottled, streaked or marbled with yellow. Foliage may become distorted. Plant may be stunted. There is no cure and the plants are best destroyed.

WILTING OR DROPPING LEAVES AND FLOWERS These symptoms are caused by incorrect cultivation or unsuitable environment. Draughts, cold conditions, gas fumes, erratic temperatures, compost too wet or excessively dry, too dry an atmosphere. Pinpoint the cause and rectify.

YELLOW LEAVES Green leaves rapidly turn yellow all over and may drop. The likely causes and remedies are the same as listed in the last entry.

37

CHAPTER FOUR

DESCRIPTIVE GUIDE TO HOUSEPLANTS

Opposite A good balance of flowering and foliage plants. Flowers are provided by a pink azalea and red poinsettia, foliage by a fatsia, dieffenbachia, pilea and selaginella

Right The zebra plant, or aphelandra, needs very warm conditions and high humidity to succeed. Don't attempt it if you cannot provide these conditions

ABOUT 100 OF THE best and most popular houseplants are described in this guide — flowering and foliage plants, bulbs, ferns, cacti and, an increasingly important group, the bromeliads (relatives of the pineapple).

The plants are listed in alphabetical order under their botanical names and the common name follows. However, for some plants the common name is the same as the botanical name, and so it has been repeated. Generally when buying from a garden centre or florist, it is sufficient to use the common name only, but if buying from a specialist grower — say of cacti or perhaps some of the more unusual bromeliads — botanical names should be used when placing an order to be absolutely certain that the plant you

receive is precisely the one you want.

After the name of the plant, general comments follow, including mention of any especially good cultivars or species. Basic cultivation requirements are then given: suitable temperature, humidity, amount of light required, general cultivation (e.g. watering, feeding, pruning if applicable), and, finally, method of propagation.

You should find all of these plants at good garden centres or florists, although for more unusual varieties and species of certain plants, or for a wider range of varieties than garden centres offer — perhaps of African violets or cacti, for example — you will need to buy from a specialist: most offer a detailed catalogue and a mail-order service.

FLOWERING PLANTS

Aphelandra squarrosa 'Louisae'
ZEBRA PLANT

This shrubby plant has large leaves which have conspicuous cream veins. Upright heads of yellow bracts are produced and last for several months.

TEMPERATURE Keep above 13°C (55°F), ideally at 21°C (70°F).

HUMIDITY Very high humidity is needed.

LIGHT Good light needed, but shade from strong sunshine.

GENERAL CULTIVATION Water well during the growing period and keep moderately moist in winter. Soil-based compost recommended; pot-on in spring. In spring, flowered plants should be cut back to just above a pair of leaves to prevent them becoming too tall.

PROPAGATION Take cuttings in spring.

Begonia
BEGONIA

The most popular begonias are the winter-flowering 'Elatior' hybrids, though they are usually simply sold as 'winter-flowering begonias'. The plants are tuberous rooted, and although they can be kept, they are generally discarded after flowering because they are not the easiest subjects to care for on a long-term basis.

TEMPERATURE In the region of 16–21°C (60–70°F), but down to 13°C (55°F) at night.

HUMIDITY Moderate humidity is needed, but if this is too high, mildew can be a problem.

LIGHT Good light is necessary, but shade from hot sun.

GENERAL CULTIVATION Maintain a steadily moist compost. If plants are kept after flowering, feed in summer and up to flowering time.

PROPAGATION Take cuttings in the spring.

Beloperone guttata
SHRIMP PLANT

This small shrubby plant produces clusters of pink bracts, shaped like a shrimp, containing white flowers. The flowers are produced almost continuously. Beloperone is now more correctly known as *Justicea brandegeana*.

TEMPERATURE Happy at around 21°C (70°F), but 16°C (60°F) is also suitable. In winter give the plant a rest by providing 10°C (50°F).

Right The shrimp plant is hardly ever out of flower and is one of the more easily grown houseplants

HUMIDITY Moderate humidity is needed.

LIGHT Good light, but shade from strong sun in summer.

GENERAL CULTIVATION Water well in the growing season, but keep only barely moist in winter. Feed weekly in spring and summer. Pot-on annually using soil-based compost. Young plants should be pinched out to encourage bushy growth. Large plants can be pruned back by half in winter.

PROPAGATION Take cuttings in spring or early summer.

Calceolaria
SLIPPERWORT

These are short-term pot plants which flower in spring and early summer, producing inflated, pouched flowers in many brilliant colours, often attractively spotted.

TEMPERATURE Provide cool conditions to ensure long-lasting flowers. A temperature of 10°C (50°F) is ideal, or slightly lower.

HUMIDITY Moderate humidity is needed, but do not spray the plants.

LIGHT Good light is required with shade from strong sun.

GENERAL CULTIVATION Keep compost steadily moist. Feeding is unnecessary, unless you are growing your own plants from seed, then feed fortnightly in summer.

PROPAGATION Plants can be raised from seeds obtained from seedsmen, sown in early summer. Keep young plants cool at all times.

Campanula isophylla
BELLFLOWER

This is a very tough and easy trailing perennial plant, ideal for hallways, etc. It flowers in summer and well into autumn, and produces blue or white, bell-shaped blooms. It is a good plant for hanging containers.

TEMPERATURE Around 10–16°C

(50–60°F); avoid high temperatures.

HUMIDITY Some humidity is necessary in the high temperature range.

LIGHT Good light needed but avoid hot sun.

GENERAL CULTIVATION Plenty of water required in spring and summer, but keep only barely moist in winter when plant is dormant. Feed every two weeks during the growing period. Regularly remove dead flowers. After flowering, cut stems back hard. Keep on the cool side in winter.

PROPAGATION Take cuttings in spring to replace old plants. Sow seeds in spring.

Chrysanthemum
POT CHRYSANTHEMUM

Dwarf pot chrysanthemums can be bought in bloom all the year round, and come in a wide range of colours. They are temporary plants, to be discarded after flowering.

TEMPERATURE To ensure a long display, keep plants cool at all times. They do not mind a temperature as low as 5°C (40°F)

HUMIDITY Slight humidity is beneficial during very warm weather.

LIGHT Good light needed.

Above The bellflower, or campanula, flowers profusely in summer and autumn and is a particularly useful plant for hanging containers in cool rooms, as it is almost hardy

GENERAL CULTIVATION Keep the compost steadily moist. No feeding necessary.

PROPAGATION Not applicable.

Clivia miniata
KAFFIR LILY

This plant produces, from thick fleshy roots, strap-shaped leaves and heads of trumpet-shaped flowers in orange or orange-red during spring.

TEMPERATURE Around 16°C (60°F) is ideal but in winter provide 10°C (50°F) to give the plant a rest.

HUMIDITY Slight humidity is necessary in warm conditions.

LIGHT Good light needed, including some sun.

GENERAL CULTIVATION Provide plenty of water in spring and summer, less in autumn, and keep only barely moist in winter. Feed fortnightly in spring and summer. Do not pot-on until the plant becomes pot-bound, and use soil-based compost. Pot-on just as plant is starting to produce flower stems. Remove dead flower heads.

PROPAGATION Remove rooted offsets when potting-on and pot-up separately.

Below The spring-flowering Kaffir lily flowers most freely when it is pot-bound, unlike most other plants

Cyclamen
SOWBREAD

The cyclamen flowers in autumn and winter, when plants are freely available, in shades of red, pink and white. Most people treat them as temporary plants, although they can be kept for many years, as they grow from a tuber. Many have large flowers, and the miniature cultivars are also exceedingly attractive.

TEMPERATURE Fairly cool, around 13–16°C (55–60°F) is ideal.

HUMIDITY Moderate, but do not spray plants.

LIGHT Maximum light required.

GENERAL CULTIVATION Do not over-water — water only when the compost is becoming dry. Avoid wetting the plant's centre or it may rot. Remove dead flowers and any yellowing leaves. If you want to keep plants after flowering, rest them from late spring to late summer by keeping the compost dry.

PROPAGATION Seeds are obtainable from seedsmen. Sow in late summer to bloom the following year.

Euphorbia pulcherrima
POINSETTIA

This very popular Christmas-flowering pot plant produces large colourful 'bracts' (these are modified leaves, not flowers). The most popular colour is red, but plants with pink or cream bracts are also available. Plants are dwarf and compact, though this is not their natural habit. They are given special treatment by the nurserymen. Best treated as temporary plants.

TEMPERATURE Best results obtained at 16°C (60°F).

HUMIDITY A little humidity is beneficial.

LIGHT Good light essential.

GENERAL CULTIVATION The compost should be allowed to dry out partially between waterings. No feeding necessary.

PROPAGATION Not applicable.

Gerbera
BARBERTON DAISY

The new dwarf, free-flowering cultivar 'Happipot', with its large, daisy flowers in a wide range of colours, produced during summer, is destined to become as popular as the dwarf pot chrysanthemums. It is a perennial plant.

TEMPERATURE Minimum of 7°C (45°F) needed.

HUMIDITY Dryish atmosphere preferred.

LIGHT Needs good light but shade from very hot sun.

GENERAL CULTIVATION Likes an airy atmosphere. Compost should be kept only slightly moist, and dryish in winter. Feed fortnightly in summer.

PROPAGATION Seeds are now available from several well-known seedsmen. Sow any time in spring.

Hydrangea
POT HYDRANGEA

These shrubby, deciduous plants flower during spring and summer, in shades of blue, purple, pink, red or white. Most people treat them as temporary plants, because it is not easy, in the home, to get them into flower again. However, they are hardy plants, so could be planted in the garden after flowering.

TEMPERATURE Keep as cool as possible — a temperature range of 10–16°C (50–60°F) is acceptable.

HUMIDITY High humidity recommended for long-lasting flowers.

LIGHT Good light ideal, but will tolerate some shade. Keep shaded from strong sunshine.

GENERAL CULTIVATION Needs plenty of water in the growing season, and feeding every two weeks during the same period.

Above Invaluable for autumn and winter flowers, the cyclamen is available in many colours, and often the foliage is attractively marbled with silver

PROPAGATION Take cuttings in spring or early summer.

Impatiens
BUSY LIZZIE

These are very popular perennial plants flowering throughout summer and into autumn. They are generally discarded after flowering, but new plants are easily produced from cuttings. The *I. wallerana* hybrids are the best known, with flowers in a wide range of colours. Even more attractive are the New Guinea hybrids with colourful leaves and flowers in shades of red and orange.

TEMPERATURE Suitable for a temperature of 21°C (70°F), but 13°C (55°F) is tolerated.

HUMIDITY Provide plenty of humidity in warm conditions.

LIGHT Good light needed, including some sun, but take care to prevent strong sun scorching the foliage.

GENERAL CULTIVATION Plenty of water needed in the growing season (the compost must not dry out) but keep only slightly moist in winter. Feed fortnightly while in active growth. Remove dead flowers regularly.

PROPAGATION Take cuttings in spring or summer. These will root in water.

Right Busy Lizzies flower continuously throughout summer and into autumn. They are easily raised from cuttings rooted in jars of water

Jasminum polyanthum
JASMINE

A popular climber that has white, sweetly scented flowers in spring.

TEMPERATURE This plant is almost hardy, so keep it cool — a maximum of 16°C (60°F), which can drop to as low as 5°C (40°F) in winter.

HUMIDITY Jasmine needs moderate humidity, and appreciates spraying in summer.

LIGHT Very good light is necessary and ideally some sun, but make sure foliage is not scorched.

GENERAL CULTIVATION Pot-on after flowering until growing in a final pot size of 20cm (8in). Prune after flowering — old shoots can be reduced by half to two-thirds. Keep compost steadily moist, but after flowering rest the plant for several weeks by reducing watering. Feed in summer and autumn.

PROPAGATION Take cuttings in summer.

Right An invaluable climber for a cool room, *Jasminum polyanthum*, or jasmine, has deliciously fragrant blooms

Pelargonium domesticum
REGAL PELARGONIUM

These free-flowering perennials produce their blooms in many colours during the summer. They can be kept for a number of years but, for best results, replace with young plants from cuttings every couple of years.

TEMPERATURE About 16°C (60°F) during spring and summer, and 10°C (50°F) during winter.

HUMIDITY Dry air is necessary. Do not wet the leaves.

LIGHT Plenty of sun needed to encourage flowering.

GENERAL CULTIVATION Stand plants out of doors for the summer after flowering. Take indoors again in early autumn. Water well during growing season, keep only barely moist in winter. Feed fortnightly in spring and summer. Best to pot-on in soil-based compost, in early spring.

PROPAGATION Take cuttings in late summer.

Primula
PRIMROSES

Highly popular short-term pot plants, discarded after flowering. The flowering period is between late autumn and late spring. Various kinds are available: *P. obconica*, *P. malacoides* (the fairy primrose), the yellow-flowered *P. × kewensis*, and the 'coloured primroses' or strains of our own native primrose, which are becoming exceedingly popular. These are available in a very wide range of colours.

TEMPERATURE Cool, between 13 and 16°C (55 and 60°F).

HUMIDITY Moderate humidity is needed for a long flowering period.

LIGHT Provide maximum light.

GENERAL CULTIVATION Keep compost steadily moist, but try not to wet foliage. Remove dead flowers regularly. Feeding is unnecessary.

PROPAGATION Seed of all varieties is available from seedsmen. Sow early to late spring. Grow young plants in cool conditions.

Above Azaleas need to be kept as cool as possible, when their winter and spring flowers will last for a long time

Rhododendron
AZALEA

These dwarf, shrubby evergreen plants flower in winter and spring, in a wide range of pink, red, purple or mauve shades, plus white.

TEMPERATURE Keep plants cool as they are nearly hardy. An ideal temperature range is 13–16°C (55–60°F) but lower temperatures are tolerated.

HUMIDITY Plants need high humidity.

LIGHT Good light required, but provide shade from strong sun.

GENERAL CULTIVATION Azaleas are lime haters and need acid compost and watering with 'soft' or rain water. Never allow the compost to dry out. Feed in summer. Stand the plants in a shady place out of doors in summer.

PROPAGATION Take cuttings in spring or early summer, but these are not easy to root.

Left The fairy primrose, or *Primula malacoides*, also needs very cool conditions. It is a favourite winter-flowering pot plant, lasting for many weeks

Saintpaulia
AFRICAN VIOLET

These are among the most popular flowering houseplants, forming neat rosettes of leaves and producing flowes in pink, red, purple, blue, white and bicoloured. Many of the modern cultivars are more easily grown and flowered than older kinds, and indeed the new Endurance strain can be grown in a temperature of 13°C (55°F). Miniature strains are also being bred, as well as microminiatures like 'Pip Squeek'.

TEMPERATURE An all-year-round temperature of 16–18°C (60–65°F) is ideal.

HUMIDITY High humidity needed, but do not spray leaves.

LIGHT Good light is necessary, but avoid very strong sunshine.

GENERAL CULTIVATION Grow in small pots, keep moderately moist between mid-spring and early autumn, drier in winter. Feed fortnightly.

PROPAGATION Take leaf cuttings in spring or summer.

Senecio × hybridus
CINERARIA

Among the most popular of the temporary houseplants (discarded after flowering), cinerarias carry large heads of daisy-like flowers in many colours, during winter and spring.

TEMPERATURE Keep on the cool side — maximum of 13–16°C (55–60°F), but this can drop to 10°C (50°F) at night.

HUMIDITY Moderate humidity is beneficial.

LIGHT Good light needed. These are ideal plants for a windowsill.

GENERAL CULTIVATION Do not allow compost to dry out — keep steadily moist. No feeding necessary. Remove dead flowers regularly.

PROPAGATION Plants are fairly easily raised from seeds sown from mid-spring to early summer. Keep young plants in cool conditions.

Sinningia speciosa
GLOXINIA

These plants grow from tubers and produce bell-shaped, red, pink, purple or white flowers in summer. They can be kept for a number of years.

TEMPERATURE Provide a minimum of 16°C (60°F).

HUMIDITY High humidity required, but do not spray plants.

LIGHT Good light needed, but provide shade from hot sun.

GENERAL CULTIVATION Keep compost steadily moist but avoid making it wet. Gradually dry off in the autumn and keep dry over winter. Re-start into growth in early spring. Feed every two weeks in the summer. Remove dead flowers regularly.

PROPAGATION Take leaf cuttings in summer.

Solanum capsicastrum
WINTER CHERRY

These popular shrubby plants produce orange or red berries in winter. They are generally treated as short-term pot plants and discarded after flowering.

TEMPERATURE Ideally around 13–16°C (55–60°F).

HUMIDITY At this temperature provide reasonably high humidity. Leaves can be sprayed daily.

Left As gloxinias grow from tubers they can be kept for many years if carefully overwintered. They bloom during the summer and colours include red, pink, purple and white. Some have bicoloured flowers

Opposite African violets need warmth and high humidity. Often they succeed in bathrooms and kitchens

LIGHT   Good light needed.

GENERAL CULTIVATION Keep the compost steadily moist. Generally no feeding is necessary.

PROPAGATION From seed, but difficult to get seedlings to produce berries in the home.

Streptocarpus
CAPE PRIMROSE

These perennial plants flower throughout summer and into autumn. The violet-blue 'Constant Nymph' is well known. Also worth obtaining are the John Innes hybrids, each with a girl's name, in a wide range of colours. All have funnel-shaped flowers and are easily grown.

TEMPERATURE Tolerates a wide temperature range, but 16–18°C (60–65°F) is ideal. Provide 10°C (50°F) during the winter rest period.

HUMIDITY Moderate humidity is needed during growing period.

LIGHT Good light, but shade from strong sunshine.

GENERAL CULTIVATION Keep steadily moist in the growing season, and dryish during the winter. Feed every two weeks in summer. Remove dead blooms regularly.

PROPAGATION Take leaf cuttings, divide the plants, or sow seeds.

Below The John Innes hybrids of streptocarpus, or Cape primrose, are well worth obtaining – they all have girls' names and come in a range of colours

FOLIAGE PLANTS

Aglaonema
CHINESE EVERGREENS

These perennial plants have large, long, pointed leaves, which may be plain green or marked with silver, grey, cream or white. Several species are offered, including *A. commutatum* and *A. modestum*. There are several well-marked cultivars of the former.

TEMPERATURE A suitable temperature is 16°C (60°F) with a minimum of 13°C (55°F).

HUMIDITY High humidity needed for luxuriant growth. Spray the leaves daily.

LIGHT Shade-loving plants, so avoid exposing them to strong sunshine. Ideal for shady corners.

GENERAL CULTIVATION Water well in the growing season, but allow the compost to become fairly dry between waterings in autumn and winter. Feed weekly in the growing season. Only pot-on when slightly pot-bound. Will not tolerate draughty places or gas fumes.

PROPAGATION Divide plants in spring, or propagate from stem sections.

Araucaria excelsa (A. heterophylla)
NORFOLK ISLAND PINE

This is naturally a large tree, but when pot grown, growth is slow and the ultimate height will be around 2m (6ft). Bright green needles are carried on horizontal branches and it looks something like a Christmas tree. It is an ideal specimen plant.

TEMPERATURE Tolerates a wide range, 7–16°C (45–60°F).

HUMIDITY A moist atmosphere is needed, particularly in warm conditions.

LIGHT A suitable plant for shade which is not too heavy. Protect from strong sunshine.

GENERAL CULTIVATION Water well in spring and summer, and keep only barely moist in winter, especially in a low

temperature. Feed every two weeks in the growing season. Pot-on each year in spring to a final pot size of 20cm (8in).

PROPAGATION Can be raised from seeds, but this is very slow.

Asparagus densiflorus 'Sprengeri'
ASPARAGUS FERN

The asparagus fern is not a true fern, but a trailing plant with fine, ferny growth, ideal for hanging baskets or for edging a group of plants.

TEMPERATURE Try to provide 16°C (60°F) with a minimum of 13°C (55°F).

HUMIDITY Growth is best in a humid atmosphere. The leaves can be sprayed with water.

LIGHT Will grow in moderate shade. Avoid exposing the plant to hot sun.

GENERAL CULTIVATION Water generously in spring and summer, but keep only slightly moist in autumn and winter.

Feed once a week in the growing season. Pot-on yearly as growth is vigorous.

PROPAGATION Divide plants in spring.

Aspidistra elatior
CAST-IRON PLANT

The cast-iron plant produces luxuriant, deep green leaves when properly cared for. It will tolerate neglect but the plant will not look so attractive. This was a favourite plant of the Victorians. There is a much rarer, variegated cultivar which is sometimes available.

TEMPERATURE Ideally about 16°C (60°F), but will tolerate 10°C (50°F) at night. It can cope with draughts.

HUMIDITY Moderate humidity desirable. The leaves can be sprayed daily in the growing season.

LIGHT Will tolerate heavy shade, but growth is better in light shade. Ideal for a dark hall or passageway.

Below There can be few more tolerant houseplants than the aspidistra. Although this foliage plant will take a great deal of neglect, there is no doubt growth will be better with adequate care

GENERAL CULTIVATION Plenty of water needed in the growing season, but water only when drying out in autumn and winter. Feed about once a month in the growing season. Pot-on annually.

PROPAGATION Divide plants in spring.

Begonia
BEGONIA

Several begonias are grown for their large, colourful foliage: *B. rex* in various cultivars has leaves patterned in several colours, including pink, red, silver, white and purple; and *B. masoniana*, the iron cross begonia, has large, rough green leaves with a large bronze-purple cross in the centre.

TEMPERATURE Ideally 21°C (70°F), but will tolerate 16°C (60°F); must not drop below 10°C (50°F).

HUMIDITY Very high humidity needed, especially in warm conditions. Do not spray leaves.

LIGHT Prefers indirect light, and will be happy in slight shade.

GENERAL CULTIVATION Water only when the compost is drying out, and keep barely moist in winter. Feed every two weeks in summer. Pot-on only when slightly pot-bound.

PROPAGATION Take leaf cuttings in spring or summer.

Caladium bicolor
ANGEL'S WINGS

One of the most beautiful of the foliage plants, caladium has paper-thin leaves coloured red, pink, white and green, depending on the cultivar. It grows from a tuber, and is perennial, the leaves dying down in the autumn. Caladium is one of the more difficult houseplants and it is essential to provide the conditions described.

TEMPERATURE A minimum of 18°C (65°F) is needed during spring and summer. When the plant is resting during the winter provide a temperature of 13°C (55°F).

HUMIDITY Must be very high throughout the growing season. Leaves can be sprayed each day with water.

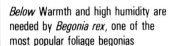

Below Warmth and high humidity are needed by *Begonia rex*, one of the most popular foliage begonias

Right Angel's wings or caladium is one of the most beautiful foliage houseplants, but it is also one of the more difficult ones to grow, needing very high temperatures and humidity

LIGHT Good light needed, but shade from strong sunshine.

GENERAL CULTIVATION Keep compost steadily moist in spring and summer. Reduce the water in autumn until the compost becomes dry and then rest the plants. Feed weekly in spring and summer. Start into growth in early spring by re-potting and resuming watering.

PROPAGATION Detach offsets when re-potting.

Calathea
PEACOCK PLANT

Two forms are offered. *Calathea makoyana* has longish leaves, attractively marked with light and dark green and silver, purple below. *C. lancifolia* (*C. insignis*), also has long leaves, purple underneath, marked with bright and deep green on the upper surface. Both are low-growing, fairly slow, perennial plants.

TEMPERATURE In the region of 16–21°C (60–70°F), but a minimum of 10°C (50°F) is needed.

HUMIDITY Provide high humidity all the year round.

LIGHT Light shade is best, and protect from strong sunshine.

GENERAL CULTIVATION Water freely in the growing season. Reduce watering in autumn and winter, but do not allow the compost to dry out. Feed every two weeks in summer, and pot-on in spring.

PROPAGATION Divide in early summer.

Chlorophytum comosum 'Variegatum'
SPIDER PLANT

Seen in most homes, this is a very adaptable plant which will take all kinds of conditions. It is grown for its grass-like, green and white striped leaves, and the small plantlets which are produced on the ends of the old flower stems.

TEMPERATURE Tolerates a wide

range, but requires a minimum of 7°C (45°F).

HUMIDITY Provide high humidity in warm conditions.

LIGHT Good light preferred, including full sun, but will also tolerate deep shade.

GENERAL CULTIVATION Water well in the growing season, but water sparingly in winter, especially in low temperatures. Feed every two weeks when in full growth. Pot-on annually in spring.

PROPAGATION Root the plantlets in small pots while they are still attached to parent. Plants can also be divided.

Cissus antarctica
KANGAROO VINE

This climber reaches a height of about 2.4m (8ft), and has fairly large, dark green serrated leaves. It is a very tough plant, tolerating draughts, fumes and dry air.

TEMPERATURE Ideally around 16°C (60°F)–21°C (70°F), but will tolerate a minimum of 4.5°C (40°F).

HUMIDITY Moderate humidity is necessary. Spray the leaves with water.

LIGHT Tolerates good light to quite deep shade and is ideal for dark hallways and passages. Avoid exposure to strong sunshine.

GENERAL CULTIVATION Let the compost dry out between waterings to

Left Calathea makoyana is popularly called the peacock plant on account of its beautifully marked leaves. It is a low-growing perennial, growth being fairly slow

prevent root rot. Feed every two weeks in summer. If plant becomes too tall, cut it back. Young plants can be pinched out to ensure plenty of stems. Pot-on annually in spring.

PROPAGATION Take cuttings in spring or early summer.

Cissus rhombifolia
GRAPE IVY

A vigorous climbing plant which grows to about 2.4m (8ft) in height, but can also be grown as a trailer. Its lobed, deep green leaves are most attractive. *Cissus rhombifolia* was formerly known as *Rhoicissus rhomboidea*.

TEMPERATURE Ideally 16°C (60°F) but a minimum of 4.5°C (40°F) is tolerated.

HUMIDITY Moderate humidity is necessary. Spray the leaves with water.

LIGHT Tolerates good light to quite deep shade. It is ideal for dark hallways and passages. Avoid exposure to strong sunshine.

GENERAL CULTIVATION Let the compost dry out between waterings to avoid root rot. Feed every two weeks in summer. If plant becomes too tall, cut it back. Young plants can be pinched out to ensure plenty of stems. Pot-on annually in spring.

PROPAGATION Take cuttings in spring or early summer.

Codiaeum
CROTON

Along with caladiums, the crotons are among the most colourful of the foliage plants, and among the most popular. Like the caladiums, they are not easy and must be given the conditions recommended for successful results. The large leathery leaves are multi-coloured: colours include red, orange, yellow, cream, copper and green, often in striking combinations of several colours.

TEMPERATURE Ideally 21°C (70°F), but a minimum of 16°C (60°F) is needed.

HUMIDITY Very high humidity needed at all times. Spray leaves with water.

LIGHT Very good light required, but avoid exposure to direct sunlight.

GENERAL CULTIVATION Water well in the growing season but only when the compost is becoming dry in winter. Feed every two weeks in spring and summer. Pot-on in spring and pinch out the tips of young plants to encourage a bushy habit. At all costs avoid draughts.

PROPAGATION Cuttings in spring. These will root in water. Alternatively, increase by air layering.

Coleus
FLAME NETTLE

These are short-term pot plants with nettle-like leaves in many bright colour combinations. They are generally discarded at the end of the growing season, because older plants are not as attractive as young specimens and tend to become leggy.

Below Among the most highly coloured foliage plants, the crotons, with their diversity of leaf shapes, are invaluable for adding interest to mixed groups of plants. They need high temperatures and humidity, so keep them in your warmest room

TEMPERATURE Around 16°C (60°F) is ideal. If the plants are kept, overwinter them at a minimum of 13°C (55°F).

HUMIDITY High humidity is needed at all times.

LIGHT Very good light is necessary for the best leaf colour, but shade from hot sun.

GENERAL CULTIVATION Keep compost steadily moist throughout the growing season and reduce watering for overwintering plants. Feed every two weeks in summer. Pot-on as required to final 15-cm (6-in) pots. The shoot tips of young plants should be pinched out to make them bushy.

PROPAGATION Take cuttings in spring or summer (will root in water), or raise your own plants from seed sown in early spring.

Cordyline terminalis
CABBAGE PALM

A palm-like plant with broad leaves which are very colourful. The leaves are usually bronzy red but the popular cultivar 'Tricolor' has pink, red and cream leaves; and 'Rededge' has red and green leaves. The plant can grow to 1m (3ft) high.

TEMPERATURE Ideally 21°C (70°F), dropping to 13–16°C (55–60°F) at night.

HUMIDITY High humidity needed.

LIGHT Good light necessary, but provide shade from strong sunshine.

GENERAL CULTIVATION Water freely in the growing season but keep compost barely moist in the winter. Feed every two weeks in summer.

PROPAGATION Take stem cuttings in spring or summer; or detach young suckers in spring, and pot-up separately.

Cyperus alternifolius
UMBRELLA PLANT

The umbrella plant has grassy stems, and leaves which radiate like the ribs of an umbrella. A small, easy, perennial plant, it likes plenty of moisture.

Schefflera actinophylla is also known as the umbrella plant, and has attractive green, hand-like leaves. It is easily grown in warm humid conditions and good light.

TEMPERATURE 16°C (60°F) is suitable but a minimum of 10°C (50°F) is needed.

HUMIDITY Provide high humidity at all times.

LIGHT Give good light, including some sun. It will tolerate shade.

GENERAL CULTIVATION Keep the plant wet throughout the year by standing the pot in a dish of water. Feed every two weeks in summer. Pot-on in spring.

PROPAGATION Divide plants in spring.

Above This is one plant you cannot overwater! The umbrella plant (cyperus) is a bog plant and the pot should be stood in a dish of water throughout the year

Right There is a probably a dumb cane in virtually every collection of houseplants, such is its popularity. Several varieties are available, the leaves of which are marked with cream or creamy yellow. It makes a good specimen plant and adds colour to a foliage group

Dieffenbachia maculata
DUMB CANE

This quick-growing, large shrubby plant, makes a good specimen plant. The large leaves are attractively marked with cream or creamy yellow. Several cultivars are available, including the popular 'Exotica'.

TEMPERATURE Ideally around 21°C (70°F), but a minimum of 16°C (60°F) is needed.

HUMIDITY Provide high humidity, including spraying leaves with water.

LIGHT Maximum light necessary for best colour but avoid exposure to strong sunshine.

GENERAL CULTIVATION Keep the compost steadily moist all the year round. Feed every two weeks in spring and summer. Pot-on each year in spring, until growing in a 30-cm (12-in) pot. Avoid draughts and fumes from gas fires.

PROPAGATION Take stem cuttings in spring and summer. Avoid getting sap near mouth and eyes as it causes severe pain and swelling.

Dizygotheca elegantissima
FALSE ARALIA

This shrubby plant is normally used as a specimen plant, and has long narrow leaves, deeply coloured copper. It is a slow grower, reaching a height of about 1.2m (4ft) in 10 years.

TEMPERATURE Ideally 16°C (60°F), but a minimum of 13°C (55°F) is necessary.

HUMIDITY High humidity is essential. Spray leaves regularly.

LIGHT Provide maximum light, but shade from strong sunshine.

GENERAL CULTIVATION Water with care: keep compost only just moist in the growing season, but allow it to dry out partially between waterings in autumn and winter. Large plants can be fed every two weeks in the growing season. Pot-on annually, and keep away from draughts.

PROPAGATION Take cuttings in spring or summer.

Dracaena
DRAGON LILY

These varied shrubs often have a palm-like habit of growth and are excellent as large specimen plants. Several cultivars are offered, like the white and green striped *D. deremensis* 'Bausei' and *D. d.* 'Warneckii'; also the *D. fragrans* cultivars with cream and green or yellow and green striped leaves.

TEMPERATURE Ideally around 21°C (70°F), but 13°C (55°F) at night is adequate.

HUMIDITY High humidity needed all year round, including spraying the leaves.

LIGHT Provide maximum light but avoid exposure to strong sunshine.

GENERAL CULTIVATION Keep plant steadily moist, except in winter when the compost should be allowed to dry out partially between waterings. Feed every two weeks. Pot-on in spring each year. Avoid draughts.

PROPAGATION Take stem cuttings in spring or summer; alternatively, propagate by air layering.

Episcia
FLAME VIOLET

These creeping or trailing plants are ideal for hanging containers. Most have silver- or bronze-striped leaves and bear tubular red or orange-red flowers in spring and summer. They are also good in a group planting or trough.

TEMPERATURE Must be kept warm at all times — 21°C (70°F) is ideal.

HUMIDITY Provide high humidity at all times.

LIGHT Good light necessary but protect from strong sun.

GENERAL CULTIVATION Water well in the growing season, but very sparingly during winter. Feed every two weeks in summer. Grow in shallow containers and use a very well-drained potting compost.

PROPAGATION Take leaf cuttings, or root the small plantlets that develop at the ends of stems.

Above Varieties of *Dracaena fragrans* are noted for their boldly striped leaves. When they reach a reasonably large size they create a dramatic effect as specimen plants in a warm room

Left The false aralia is often used as a specimen plant. It is a slow grower though, and takes about 10 years to attain sizeable proportions

x *Fatshedera lizei*
FATSHEDERA

This tough climbing plant reaches a height of 2m (6ft) and has glossy, green, hand-shaped leaves. It is a bigeneric hybrid between *Fatsia japonica* and *Hedera helix*. The plant is ideal for cool rooms and hallways and will not object to draughts.

TEMPERATURE Ideally around 16°C (60°F) but will tolerate 10°C (50°F).

HUMIDITY Moderate humidity is needed.

LIGHT Light shade is ideal, though it is tolerant of poor light conditions.

GENERAL CULTIVATION Needs ample water in growing season, but far less in winter, especially if the temperature is low. Feed every two weeks. Pot-on in spring each year. Support the stem with a moss pole or cane. Cut plant hard back if it becomes bare at the base to encourage new shoots from lower down.

PROPAGATION Take cuttings in spring or summer.

Below This is the variegated form of *Fatshedera lizei*, a tough climbing plant suited to cool rooms. Try it in a hallway as it will not object to draughts from doorways

Fatsia japonica
JAPANESE ARALIA

This hardy foliage shrub has huge hand-shaped, shiny green leaves. It makes a superb specimen plant for almost any room.

TEMPERATURE Can range from just above freezing to about 16°C (60°F). The plant is suitable for most rooms.

HUMIDITY It does not mind dry air but in higher temperatures it is best to spray the leaves daily with water.

LIGHT Tolerates very low light levels, so it is ideal for a dark hallway. Also suited to good light, but not direct sun.

GENERAL CULTIVATION Keep well watered in the growing season, but allow the compost almost to dry out between waterings in winter. Feed every two weeks in summer. To encourage branching, pinch out the tip of the young plant. Pot-on regularly in spring.

PROPAGATION Take stem cuttings in summer, or detach and pot on rooted suckers in spring.

Ficus
FIGS

These are the ornamental figs. Several kinds of trees and shrubs are offered and they all make excellent specimen plants. The weeping fig, *F. benjamina*, will reach a height of about 2m (6ft) and the arching branches bear shiny green oval leaves. The mistletoe fig, *F. deltoidea*, is a 60-cm (2-ft) high bushy plant with deep green foliage and yellow berries. The huge fiddle-back fig, *F. lyrata*, can reach a height of 2m (6ft) or more, and has large violin-shaped leaves. It is a fast grower. There are several small climbing or trailing species, too, including *F. pumila*, and *F. radicans* 'Variegata' with green and white leaves.

TEMPERATURE Ideally 16–21°C (60–70°F).

HUMIDITY The figs grow best in high humidity.

LIGHT Requires good light to slight shade. Avoid exposure to strong sun.

GENERAL CULTIVATION Keep compost moist in the growing season but drier in winter. Feed every two weeks in summer.

PROPAGATION Increase *F. benjamina* from stem cuttings or by air layering; *F. deltoidea* from stem cuttings; *F. lyrata* by air layering or from leaf-bud cuttings; and *F. pumila* and *F. radicans* from stem cuttings.

Ficus elastica
RUBBER PLANT

Found in the homes of most houseplant lovers, this tree has large, thick, deep green, glossy leaves, and is very suitable as a specimen plant.

TEMPERATURE 16–21°C (60–70°F) is ideal.

HUMIDITY Dry air is tolerated but growth is much better in high humidity.

LIGHT Good light is best, though poor light is tolerated. Protect from direct sunlight.

GENERAL CULTIVATION Keep compost steadily moist in the growing season, but allow compost to dry out between waterings in autumn and winter. Feed every two weeks in the growing season. Pot-on annually in spring. If plant becomes too tall cut out the top.

PROPAGATION Increase by leaf-bud cuttings or air layer in spring or summer.

Fittonia verschaffeltii
MOSAIC PLANT

A creeping, prostrate plant which is not too easy to grow although success should be ensured in a bottle garden. Its deep green leaves have red veins. The cultivar *F.v.* 'Argyroneura' has silver veins, and *F.v.* 'Argyroneura Nana' is very low growing.

TEMPERATURE 16–21°C (60–70°F) is required.

HUMIDITY Provide high humidity throughout the year.

LIGHT Give it a position in light shade, and avoid exposure to direct sun.

GENERAL CULTIVATION The compost must be kept only slightly moist the year round. Excess water results in stems rotting. Grow in small pots of peat-based compost and feed every two weeks in summer.

PROPAGATION Take stem cuttings in spring or summer.

Left The fiddle-back fig, *Ficus lyrata*, can reach a height of over 2m (6ft) and is a fast grower. It must have the largest leaves of any houseplant and can be used as a single specimen in a room

Below The mosaic plant, or fittonia, is an ideal subject for a bottle garden as it needs very high humidity and a steady temperature

Above An easy-going specimen plant for a cool room, the silk oak can quickly gain a height of 2m (6ft). Small plants are very useful for foliage contrast in a mixed group of plants

Bottom right Varieties of the common ivy, like 'Glacier', are extremely versatile – they can be used as trailers or climbers. They are hardy and therefore suited to cool rooms

Below Unlike the majority of houseplants, gynura or velvet plant has densely hairy leaves, which must be kept dry

Grevillea robusta
SILK OAK

This tree has attractive, ferny leaves and will quickly make a specimen plant 2m (6ft) high.

TEMPERATURE 13–18°C (55–65°F) is suitable.

HUMIDITY Provide moderate to high humidity.

LIGHT Good to medium light conditions needed.

GENERAL CULTIVATION Allow the compost to become partially dry between waterings and water sparingly in winter. Feed fortnightly in summer. Pot-on annually in spring, using a pot two sizes larger.

PROPAGATION Sow seeds in spring.

Gynura aurantiaca
VELVET PLANT

This spreading perennial plant has the most stunning leaves, which are densely covered with purple hairs.

TEMPERATURE 16°C (60°F) is ideal, but a minimum of 10°C (50°F) is needed.

HUMIDITY Provide dry air or slight humidity. Do not spray leaves.

LIGHT Good light needed, but give shade from strong sunshine.

GENERAL CULTIVATION Water well in the growing season, and keep only slightly moist in winter. Feed every two weeks when plants are in active growth. To prevent leggy growth, cut back plants in spring.

PROPAGATION Take cuttings in spring.

Hedera
IVY

The ivies are hardy plants and will therefore tolerate very cool conditions. They are also very adaptable, growing in good light or quite deep shade and although they are climbing plants they can also be used as trailers. There are many cultivars of the common ivy (*Hedera helix*), with plain green or variegated foliage. The larger leaved variegated Canary Island ivy (*H. canariensis* 'Variegata') is a very popular houseplant and requires slightly warmer conditions.

TEMPERATURE Around 10–16°C (50–60°F), although lower temperatures at night are tolerated. It will survive draughts.

HUMIDITY Provide moderate humidity for best results. Spray the leaves frequently.

LIGHT The variegated ivies need good light, but not direct sun. The green-leaved kinds will tolerate quite deep shade.

GENERAL CULTIVATION Keep the compost steadily moist in spring and

summer, but on the dry side in winter. Feed every two weeks in summer. Pot-on in spring and pinch out tips to encourage new growth.

PROPAGATION Take cuttings in spring or summer.

Heptapleurum arboricola
PARASOL PLANT

One of the newer houseplants, this tree will quickly reach a height of about 2m (6ft), and bears attractive, green, hand-like leaves. It makes an excellent specimen plant.

TEMPERATURE Ideally 21°C (70°F), but a minimum of 10°C (50°F) is needed.

HUMIDITY Best in moist atmosphere.

LIGHT Provide very good light, but protect the plant from strong sun.

GENERAL CULTIVATION Water well in the growing season, but sparingly in the autumn and winter. Feed every two weeks in the growing season. Pot on in spring. Pinch out the tips of young plants to obtain bushy specimens.

PROPAGATION Take stem cuttings in spring.

Above One of the newer houseplants, the parasol plant will quickly attain a height of about 2m (6ft) and is especially useful as a bold specimen plant in a warm room

Hypoestes phyllostachya
POLKA DOT PLANT

This dwarf bushy plant has small, oval leaves heavily spotted with pink. It is becoming popular and is quite easy to grow. Also sold as *H. sanguinolenta*.

TEMPERATURE A range of 13–18°C (55–65°F) is suitable.

HUMIDITY Provide high humidity.

LIGHT Provide very good light for the best leaf colour, but avoid very strong sunshine.

GENERAL CULTIVATION Allow the compost to dry out partially between waterings. Avoid very wet compost. Feed every two weeks in the growing period, and pot-on regularly. Young plants can have their growing tips pinched out to encourage them to grow bushy.

PROPAGATION Sow seeds in spring.

Maranta leuconeura
PRAYER PLANT

This popular, low-growing, very colourful foliage plant has leaves which move into a vertical position at night. The leaves are intricately marked with purple between bluish veins and are purple on the undersides. Cultivars include 'Erythrophylla', with red veins, and 'Kerchoveana', which is spotted red-brown. 'Massangeana' also has red veins.

TEMPERATURE 16–21°C (60–70°F)

Below The popular prayer plant, *Maranta leuconeura*, is a low grower, ideal for the front of mixed foliage groups in a warm room. At night the leaves fold upwards – hence the popular name

is suitable, minimum 10°C (50°F).

HUMIDITY Provide very high humidity all year round.

LIGHT Good light is required but protect from strong sunshine.

GENERAL CULTIVATION Keep compost steadily moist in the growing season, but allow to dry out partially between waterings in autumn and winter. Feed every two weeks in summer. Pot-on annually to a final size of 20cm (8in).

PROPAGATION Take cuttings in spring, or divide plants.

Monstera deliciosa
SWISS CHEESE PLANT

This is one of the best plants for use as a specimen, with its deeply cut and holed leaves, which are heart-shaped and uncut when young. It is a vigorous climber, and produces long aerial roots. Grow it up a moss pole, or some other support.

TEMPERATURE Ideally 16–21°C (60–70°F), but a minimum of 10°C (50°F) is needed.

HUMIDITY Provide very high humidity.

LIGHT Give light shade in the summer but maximum light in winter.

GENERAL CULTIVATION Water well in the growing season, but keep only slightly moist in winter. Feed every two weeks in spring and summer. Pot-on annually in spring.

PROPAGATION Root stem sections in spring or summer.

Chamaedorea, Howea, Neanthe
PALMS

Several palms are available, including *Chamaedorea elegans*, an easy species, slowly reaching a height of 1.2m (4ft); *Howea forsteriana*, also easy, and again slow, but growing to 2.4m (8ft); and *Neanthe elegans* (*N. bella*), up to 1m (3ft), very easy and adaptable. All palms make good specimen plants but also look attractive in mixed groups.

TEMPERATURE Around 21°C (70°F) suits all species, with a minimum of 10°C (50°F).

HUMIDITY Maintain humid conditions to prevent leaf tips going brown.

LIGHT Best in good light, but preferably not direct sun. Slight shade is also acceptable.

GENERAL CULTIVATION Give plenty of water in summer, but be very sparing in autumn and winter. Pot-on only when plants become pot-bound. Feed every two weeks in summer.

PROPAGATION Sow seeds, divide or detach rooted suckers.

Peperomia
PEPPER ELDER

These low-growing perennial plants are available with several different leaf colours and textures. A few popular ones include *P. argyreia*, with leaves banded silver and green; *P. caperata*, with deep green crinkled leaves, and *P. obtusifolia* 'Variegata', with thick, fleshy leaves variegated cream and green.

TEMPERATURE Ideally 16°C (60°F), and make sure it does not fall much below this.

HUMIDITY High humidity necessary all the year round.

LIGHT Light shade is ideal, and certainly not a position in full sun.

GENERAL CULTIVATION Never allow the compost to remain wet. Water only when it is drying out, and be very sparing in winter. Feed fortnightly in the growing season. Pot-on only when pot-bound. Peperomias do best in small pots.

PROPAGATION Take leaf cuttings (whole leaves) in spring or summer.

Philodendron
PHILODENDRON

These are among the most popular plants, with bold, often dramatic, foliage. Some species are climbers and produce aerial roots; grow these up a moss pole. Others are non-climbers. Popular philo-

dendrons include *P. bipinnatifidum*, non-climbing, with large, deeply cut leaves, height to about 1.2m (4ft); *P. angustisectum (P. elegans)*, a climber growing to 1.2m (4ft), with long, well-divided leaves; *P. erubescens*, a climber with large, arrow-shaped leaves, coppery below; *P. scandens*, the most popular and easiest climber or trailer, with small, heart-shaped leaves; and *P.* 'Burgundy', a climber with shield-shaped leaves, red below.

TEMPERATURE Ideally 21°C (70°F) is needed, with a minimum of 16°C (60°F).

HUMIDITY Provide high humidity all year round.

LIGHT Ideal for poor light conditions, but give good light in winter if possible. Avoid hot sunshine.

GENERAL CULTIVATION Water well in summer, with moderate watering in the winter. Feed every two weeks in the growing season. Pot-on in spring.

PROPAGATION Root stem sections or increase by air layering in spring or summer.

Below Chamaedorea elegans is a popular and easy-going palm, slowly attaining a height of 1.2m (4ft). This is quite an old specimen which has produced some trusses of flowers

Pilea cadierei
ALUMINIUM PLANT

This low-growing, compact plant has oval leaves heavily splashed with silver. Although perennial, plants only live for a few years. A very compact cultivar, and the one usually offered, is called 'Nana'.

TEMPERATURE Ideally 16°C (60°F) but 13°C (55°F) at night is adequate.

HUMIDITY Moderate humidity is preferable.

LIGHT A good plant for a slightly shady place, but ensure good light during winter.

GENERAL CULTIVATION Do not over-water. Keep slightly moist in the growing season, and on the dry side in winter. Feed every two weeks in summer. Young plants should be pinched out to encourage a bushy habit. Replace three-year-old plants with new ones.

PROPAGATION Take cuttings in spring.

Rhoeo spathacea (R. discolor)
MOSES-IN-THE-CRADLE

This attractive plant forms a rosette of spreading, stiff, sword-shaped leaves, which are deep green on top and bright purple beneath. Small white flowers appear between the leaves, looking like a baby in a cradle, hence the common name.

TEMPERATURE 16–21°C (60–70°F) is best, with a minimum of 13°C (55°F).

HUMIDITY High humidity needed in summer. The plant benefits from daily spraying with water.

LIGHT This is a shade-loving plant and so can be placed well into the room. Avoid exposure to strong sunshine.

GENERAL CULTIVATION Keep the compost steadily moist during the growing season. Be very sparing with water in winter, but do not allow the plant to dry out. In summer feed every two weeks. Do not use too large a pot — a 12.5-cm (5-in) pot is suitable for the final potting.

Below The aluminium plant is so called because the leaves are heavily splashed with silver. It is a highly popular foliage plant which lives for only a few years, although cuttings are easily rooted in the spring

PROPAGATION Take cuttings in spring or summer.

Sansevieria trifasciata 'Laurentii'
MOTHER-IN-LAW'S-TONGUE

A very tough and popular plant, mother-in-law's tongue has stiff, upright, sword-like leaves banded in the middle with grey and green, and broadly edged with gold. It is so adaptable, it will grow in virtually any room.

TEMPERATURE Ideally around 16–21°C (60–70°F), with a minimum of 10°C (50°F).

HUMIDITY Provide a fairly dry atmosphere.

LIGHT Very tolerant of all conditions from shade to bright sun. It grows best, though, in very good light.

GENERAL CULTIVATION Never allow the compost to remain wet; only water when the compost is dry. Feed well-established plants about once a month in summer. Pot-on in spring but only if the plant is pot-bound.

PROPAGATION Can be propagated from leaf cuttings (sections), but the young plants will not have the yellow edge. To retain the yellow banding, detach rooted offsets and repot.

Saxifraga stolonifera
MOTHER OF THOUSANDS

This is a hardy plant, forming a rosette of rounded, deep green leaves, with silvery veins and purple undersides. The plant produces many long thin stems, on the ends of which are tiny plants. This makes the plant ideal for use in hanging containers. It may also be sold as *S. sarmentosa*.

TEMPERATURE In the growing season, around 16°C (60°F) is suitable, but lower — around 4.5°C (40°F) — in winter.

HUMIDITY A humid atmosphere is preferable, particularly in higher temperatures.

LIGHT Ideal plant for shade, but will take good light provided it is not placed in a position in strong sunshine.

GENERAL CULTIVATION Keep compost steadily moist in the growing season, but water only when the compost is dry in the autumn and winter. Feed every two weeks in summer.

PROPAGATION Root plantlets in small pots while they are still attached to the parent.

Scindapsus aureus
DEVIL'S IVY

This popular climber has heart-shaped leaves, and is ideal for training to a moss pole, or it can be used as a trailer. The leaves are green, marked with yellow. There are also available cream and yellow variegated cultivars.

TEMPERATURE Ideally around 21°C (70°F), but not below 16°C (60°F)

HUMIDITY High humidity recommended at all times. Spraying the leaves is beneficial.

LIGHT Provide bright light for the best variegation, but it will tolerate poor light and even quite deep shade. Keep out of strong sun.

GENERAL CULTIVATION Water with care: keep slightly moist in the growing season, and only barely moist in autumn and winter. Feed every two weeks in the growing season. Pot-on every spring.

PROPAGATION Take cuttings or stem sections in spring or summer.

Spathiphyllum wallisii
WHITE SAILS

This plant could be included under the heading foliage or flowering houseplants, because it is attractive in both respects. It is a low-growing perennial with glossy, long leaves, and pure white arum-like flowers which appear in spring or summer. 'Mauna Loa' is a slightly taller cultivar.

TEMPERATURE Ideally around 16°C (60°F), but a minimum of 13°C (55°F) is needed.

HUMIDITY High humidity required.

Above The mother-in-law's tongue is among the top ten houseplants. So adaptable is it that it will thrive in virtually any room. It grows best in very good light and a dryish atmosphere

LIGHT Provide good light but protect from full sun.

GENERAL CULTIVATION Water well in the growing season, and keep only slightly moist in autumn and winter. Feed every two weeks in the growing season. Pot-on annually in spring.

PROPAGATION Divide in spring.

Syngonium podophyllum
GOOSE FOOT, ARROWHEAD

This small climbing plant has attractive arrow-shaped leaves. The cultivar 'Albolineatum' has leaves marked with silver, and 'Green Gold' is yellow and green. It is suitable for growing in hanging containers.

TEMPERATURE 21°C (70°F) is ideal, but a minimum of 16°C (60°F) is needed.

HUMIDITY Provide moderate humidity. Spray leaves with water.

LIGHT Tolerates bright light or slight shade, but avoid contact with strong sun.

GENERAL CULTIVATION Keep the compost steadily moist the year round. Feed every two weeks in summer. Can be trained up a moss pole.

PROPAGATION Take cuttings or stem sections in spring or summer.

Tolmiea menziesii
PICK-A-BACK PLANT

This compact perennial has green heart-shaped leaves, which carry young plants at their bases. It is a useful plant for very cool rooms and makes a good hanging basket plant.

TEMPERATURE A range of 7–16°C (45–60°F) is suitable.

HUMIDITY Provide slight humidity.

LIGHT Suitable for light shade.

GENERAL CULTIVATION Water moderately the year round. Feed fortnightly in the growing season. Pot-on in spring. Raise new plants regularly to replace old ones.

PROPAGATION Root young plantlets into small pots while they are still attached to the parent plant.

Tradescantia and *Zebrina*
WANDERING JEW

These very popular trailing plants are ideal for hanging baskets or the edges of group plantings. There are several kinds of tradescantia, generally with variegated or striped leaves. The most striking cultivar, though, is 'Quicksilver', striped silvery white. *Zebrina pendula* is banded silver and the undersides of the leaves are purple.

TEMPERATURE 16–21°C (60–70°F) ideal, minimum of 10°C (50°F).

HUMIDITY High humidity recommended, though not essential.

LIGHT Provide good light.

GENERAL CULTIVATION Water well in the growing season, and keep only slightly moist in autumn and winter. Feed fortnightly when in full growth. Pot-on annually, pinch out tips of stems for bushy specimens.

PROPAGATION Take cuttings in spring or summer. They can be rooted in water.

Yucca elephantipes
SPINELESS YUCCA

This plant has recently become extremely popular, and is good as a specimen plant. Its long, upright, sword-shaped leaves are carried at the top of a bare trunk.

TEMPERATURE 13–18°C (55–65°F).

HUMIDITY Dryish atmosphere.

LIGHT Good light needed, including some sun.

GENERAL CULTIVATION Water well in the growing season, but very sparingly in autumn and winter. Feed every two weeks in the growing season. It is a heavy plant, so use soil-based compost and a clay pot.

PROPAGATION Small offsets may appear at the base and these can be detached and rooted in the spring.

Opposite Goose foot or arrowhead is a small climbing plant, available in several varieties, whose leaves may be marked with silver or yellow. It is also an excellent subject for hanging containers. High temperatures and moderate humidity will keep the plant happy

FERNS

Adiantum raddianum
MAIDENHAIR FERN

These are dainty, black-stemmed ferns with tiny, pale green, fan-shaped leaflets.

TEMPERATURE   Ideally   16–18°C (60–65°F) all year round.

HUMIDITY   Provide high humidity, but do not spray leaves.

LIGHT   Good light required, but avoid exposure to direct sunlight.

GENERAL CULTIVATION   Keep the compost steadily moist, but reduce watering if kept in cool conditions. Feed fortnightly in the spring and summer. Only repot (in spring) if pot-bound.

PROPAGATION   Divide in spring.

Below The holly fern is tough and adaptable, being suited to cool rooms and thriving in good or poor light. Unlike some ferns it does not require high humidity to succeed

Asplenium bulbiferum
MOTHER FERN

The mother fern has attractive feathery fronds on black stalks. The leaflets carry tiny plantlets, hence the common name.

TEMPERATURE   A minimum of 13°C (55°F) is needed.

HUMIDITY   Provide low to moderate humidity.

LIGHT   Good light is required, but avoid direct sunlight. Slight shade is tolerated.

GENERAL CULTIVATION   Keep it steadily moist all year round, and feed fortnightly in summer. Pot-on as soon as pot is full of roots, in the spring.

PROPAGATION   Pick off plantlets, and plant in a seed tray. When well rooted, pot-off.

Cyrtomium falcatum
HOLLY FERN

A very tough and adaptable fern with 60-cm (2-ft) long fronds bearing deep green, shiny, pointed leaflets.

TEMPERATURE   10–16°C (50–60°F) is suitable.

HUMIDITY   Provide low humidity.

LIGHT   Good light preferable, but will take shady conditions. Avoid exposure to direct sunlight.

GENERAL CULTIVATION   In higher temperatures keep the compost steadily moist but reduce watering in low temperatures. Feed every two weeks in growing period. Pot-on when plants are pot-bound.

PROPAGATION   Divide in spring.

Nephrolepis exaltata
SWORD FERN

This fern has arching, light green, deeply cut fronds, and is ideal for hanging containers, where it quickly develops into a luxuriant specimen.

TEMPERATURE   Try to maintain a

temperature of 16°C (60°F) all year round.

HUMIDITY High humidity is necessary. Spray daily.

LIGHT Good light needed but do not expose to strong sunlight.

GENERAL CULTIVATION Keep the compost steadily moist. Feed every two weeks in spring and summer. Pot-on in spring if pot-bound.

PROPAGATION This fern produces runners and the tips of these can be removed and rooted.

Platycerium bifurcatum
STAG'S HORN FERN

In the wild, this is a tree-dwelling (epiphytic) fern. The large fronds are shaped like antlers. There are also 'clasping' fronds which grow around the container or support, and these eventually turn brown. Also sold as *P. alcicorne*.

TEMPERATURE Maintain 16–18°C (60–65°F).

HUMIDITY High humidity needed. Spray leaves daily.

LIGHT Good light is necessary, but avoid exposure to direct sunlight.

GENERAL CULTIVATION Although it is sold in pots, it is best grown on a piece of bark with the roots covered with sphagnum moss. Hold the plant in place with nylon thread. Hang in a suitable position. Water by placing the bark and roots in water about once a week. Feed every four weeks in the growing season.

PROPAGATION Remove offsets in spring.

Pteris cretica
RIBBON FERN

The fronds of the ribbon fern are rather unusual, divided into long narrow leaflets. It grows to a height of 45cm (18in). The cultivar 'Albo-lineata' has cream-striped leaflets.

TEMPERATURE A minimum of 16°C (60°F) is needed.

HUMIDITY High humidity is needed.

LIGHT Provide good light, but avoid exposure to direct sunlight.

GENERAL CULTIVATION Keep the compost steadily moist at all times but avoid waterlogging it. Feed every two weeks in spring and summer. Pot-on only when slightly pot-bound, in spring.

PROPAGATION Divide in spring.

BROMELIADS

Aechmea fasciata
URN PLANT

Probably the most popular bromeliad of all, this plant forms a tall rosette of broad, recurved, grey-green banded leaves. The leaves form a vase, which should be kept filled with fresh water. Blue or lilac flowers are produced among pink bracts.

TEMPERATURE Ideally 16°C (60°F) and above, but a minimum of 10°C (50°F) is needed.

HUMIDITY Requires very high humidity, although less in cool conditions.

LIGHT Good light needed, but shaded from direct sunlight.

GENERAL CULTIVATION Keep the compost moist, but not saturated, all year round. Feed about once a month in spring and summer. Use small pots and pot-on only when pot-bound. Use a peat-based compost (well drained) or a mixture of equal parts peat and leafmould.

PROPAGATION Remove and pot-on the offsets in spring or summer.

Ananas comosus 'Variegatus'
PINEAPPLE

This ornamental pineapple forms a wide-spreading rosette of narrow, spiny, green leaves, widely edged with cream. It will form a reddish fruit after flowering.

TEMPERATURE As for *Aechmea.*

HUMIDITY As for *Aechmea.*

LIGHT Very good light and even direct sunlight is needed for the best colour.

GENERAL CULTIVATION Moderate watering, and in winter only enough to prevent compost drying out. Feed monthly in spring and summer. Pot-on every two years, using a soil-based compost with extra peat. Clay pots recommended.

PROPAGATION Remove and pot-on the suckers in summer.

Billbergia nutans
QUEEN'S TEARS

This epiphyte forms a clump of arching, deep green, narrow leaves. The small flowers are green, pink and blue, surrounded by pink bracts.

Right Aechmea fasciata, the urn plant, is probably the most popular of all the bromeliads. It is generally bought in flower and the flower head can last for at least six months. Keep the 'vase' filled with fresh water

TEMPERATURE As for *Aechmea*.

HUMIDITY As for *Aechmea*.

LIGHT As for *Aechmea*.

GENERAL CULTIVATION As for *Aechmea*.

PROPAGATION Divide or remove offsets in spring.

Cryptanthus
EARTH STAR

Earth stars produce flat rosettes of leaves, which may be striped, barred or mottled with various colours.

TEMPERATURE Ideally 16°C (60°F) and above, but a minimum of 10°C (50°F) is needed.

HUMIDITY Very high humidity essential, less in cool conditions.

LIGHT Good light needed, but shaded from direct sunlight.

GENERAL CULTIVATION Keep the compost moist, but not wet, all year round. Feed about once a month in spring and summer. Use small pots and pot-on only when pot-bound. Use peat-based compost (well drained) or a mixture of equal parts peat and leafmould.

PROPAGATION Remove and pot-on the offsets in spring or summer.

Guzmannia lingulata
GUZMANNIA

This epiphyte produces a spreading rosette of shiny green leaves finely striped with purple and striking orange or red flower spikes. Keep the central vase filled with fresh water.

TEMPERATURE As for *Aechmea*.

HUMIDITY As for *Aechmea*.

LIGHT As for *Aechmea*.

GENERAL CULTIVATION As for *Aechmea*.

PROPAGATION Remove and pot-on the offsets in spring or summer.

Nidularium fulgens
BLUSHING BROMELIAD

An epiphyte, forming a low spreading rosette, the leaves making a vase which should be kept filled with fresh water. The leaves are shiny, green, mottled deeper green and bright red at the base, which gives a red centre to the plant. The flower spike is composed of bright red bracts and violet-blue flowers.

TEMPERATURE As for *Aechmea*.

HUMIDITY As for *Aechmea*.

LIGHT As for *Aechmea*.

GENERAL CULTIVATION As for *Aechmea*.

PROPAGATION Remove and pot-on the offsets in spring or summer.

Epiphytic *Tillandsia*
AIR PLANTS

These small tree- or rock-dwelling (epiphytic) plants are now creating much interest and are available from many garden centres. They cannot be grown in

Above There are lots of cryptanthus, or earth stars, available. This one is *C. zonatus*. Unlike many of the bromeliads, cryptanthus grows in soil in the wild, so will be perfectly happy in pots

pots as they produce few, if any, roots and in any case would rot off. Plants must be grown on wood, such as driftwood or mangrove root, or on cork bark. Gently wedge plants into nooks and crannies, or tie into place with clear nylon thread.

These plants absorb moisture through grey scales on their leaves. They come in varied shapes, from the bulbous with contorted leaves (*T. caput-medusae, T. butzii, T. baileyi*), rush-like (*T. juncea*), contorted rosettes (*T. ionantha*), fine-leaved and silvery (*T. argentea*), to the strands of Spanish moss (*T. usneoides*).

TEMPERATURE   Minimum not below 10°C (50°F) but ideally provide 16°C (60°F) and above.

HUMIDITY   High humidity required.

LIGHT   Provide good indirect light.

GENERAL CULTIVATION   Water by light mist spraying daily in high temperatures, or weekly if the temperature drops down to 10°C (50°F). Use rainwater if tap water is 'hard'. Plenty of fresh air needed. Feed in spring and summer with one-quarter strength houseplant fertilizer, once a month.

PROPAGATION   From the offsets that replace the parent plant, which dies after flowering.

Tillandsia cyanea
PINK QUILL

An epiphyte, pink quill forms an arching rosette of narrow, pointed, green leaves. The flowers are blue with pink bracts.

TEMPERATURE   As for *Aechmea.*

HUMIDITY   As for *Aechmea.*

LIGHT   As for *Aechmea.*

GENERAL CULTIVATION   As for *Aechmea.*

PROPAGATION   Remove and pot-on the offsets in spring or summer.

Vriesia splendens
FLAMING SWORD

An epiphytic (tree-dwelling) bromeliad, its rosette of deep green, brown-banded leaves forming a vase, which should be kept filled with fresh water. The flower head is a scarlet spike of bracts with yellow flowers.

TEMPERATURE   As for *Aechmea.*

HUMIDITY   As for *Aechmea.*

LIGHT   As for *Aechmea.*

GENERAL CULTIVATION   As for *Aechmea.*

PROPAGATION   Remove and pot-on the offsets in spring or summer.

Below The flaming sword, or *Vriesia splendens*, forms a 'vase' which should be kept filled with fresh water. It is normally bought in flower

BULBS

Crocus
CROCUS

The large-flowered Dutch crocuses flower in spring, and the best for growing indoors are the blue, white or striped cultivars.

TEMPERATURE Keep as cool as possible after potting until shoots appear. Then ideally provide a maximum of no more than 10°C (50°F).

HUMIDITY Normal room conditions are suitable.

LIGHT After potting keep corms in complete darkness until shoots are about 12mm (½in) high. Then give full light.

GENERAL CULTIVATION Pot corms in early to mid-autumn, using bulb fibre. A 15-cm (6-in) diameter bulb bowl will hold eight corms. Only just cover the corms with fibre. Keep moist at all times. Plant corms outdoors after flowering.

PROPAGATION Remove cormlets from around the base of the corms when the leaves turn brown, and grow on outdoors.

Gloriosa rothschildiana
GLORY LILY

This tender climbing lily grows from a tuber. Crimson and yellow flowers are produced in summer and early autumn.

TEMPERATURE Maintain 21°C (70°F) during the growing season, 13–16°C (55–60°F) when dormant.

HUMIDITY High humidity required in growing season.

LIGHT Good light needed during growing season.

GENERAL CULTIVATION Pot tubers in late winter or early spring, one in each 15-cm (6-in) pot, using soil-based compost. Buds should just protrude above the compost. Train stems to canes. Keep compost steadily moist. After flowering, reduce water, and when stems have died cut them down and stop watering. Repot the tubers in fresh compost during the

following late winter or early spring.

PROPAGATION Remove and pot offsets when repotting.

Hippeastrum
HIPPEASTRUM

A tender long-lived bulb which produces in spring or early summer huge, trumpet-shaped flowers in various shades of red, orange, pink and white.

TEMPERATURE Maintain 16°C (60°F) in growing season, and keep just frost free over winter rest period.

HUMIDITY Normal room conditions are suitable.

LIGHT Needs maximum light when growing.

GENERAL CULTIVATION The bulbs are generally available in autumn. Pot one to each 15-cm (6-in) pot, using soil-based compost, and leave the upper part of the bulb exposed. Keep compost slightly moist. Feed every two weeks after flowering and place in sun if possible. In autumn, as leaves die down, reduce and finally stop watering. Store

Above The climbing glory lily grows from a tuber, which can be kept from year to year. The spectacular flowers are produced in summer and early autumn. It likes warm conditions and humidity

Above Hyacinths can be had in flower at Christmas time if specially treated bulbs are planted in early autumn. Many varieties are highly scented and various colours are available

dry in frost-proof place over winter. Restart into growth in late winter. Repot every three or four years.

PROPAGATION Remove and pot bulbils when repotting.

Hyacinthus
HYACINTHS

Hyacinths are popular hardy bulbs for winter or spring flowering. Specially treated bulbs flower in time for Christmas. Many colours are available and most cultivars are highly scented.

TEMPERATURE After potting, keep as cool as possible. When shoots are 5cm (2in) high, place in a temperature of 10°C (50°F). When flower buds have formed, increase to 16°C (60°F).

HUMIDITY Normal room conditions are suitable.

LIGHT After potting, keep in complete darkness until shoots are 5cm (2in) high, then give full light.

GENERAL CULTIVATION Pot bulbs in early autumn, using bulb fibre. A 15-cm (6-in) bulb bowl will take three bulbs — leave top third of each bulb exposed. Keep fibre steadily moist. Flower spikes will need thin canes to support them. Plant outdoors after flowering.

PROPAGATION Not applicable.

Narcissus
DAFFODILS

Use specially prepared bulbs for winter flowering. Try cultivars like 'Golden Harvest', 'Grand Soleil d'Or', and 'Paper White'.

TEMPERATURE As cool as possible after potting. When the shoots have reached a height of 2.5cm (1in) provide 10°C (50°F), and raise to 16°C (60°F) when flower buds have formed.

HUMIDITY Normal room conditions are suitable.

LIGHT After potting keep bulbs in complete darkness until shoots appear (about 2.5cm [or 1in] high), then provide full light.

GENERAL CULTIVATION Pot bulbs in early to mid-autumn, using bulb fibre. The tips of the bulbs should just be exposed. A 30-cm (12-in) bulb bowl will hold six bulbs. Keep fibre moist at all times. Plant outdoors after flowering but discard 'Grand Soleil d'Or' and 'Paper White'.

PROPAGATION Remove offsets when lifting bulbs in late spring.

Tulipa
TULIPS

These hardy bulbs are also available specially prepared for Christmas flowering. Otherwise, use early-flowering cultivars. Many colours are available.

TEMPERATURE As for hyacinths.

HUMIDITY Normal room conditions are suitable.

LIGHT As for hyacinths.

GENERAL CULTIVATION Pot bulbs in early autumn, using bulb fibre. A 15-cm (6-in) bulb bowl will hold five bulbs. Pot so that the tops of the bulbs are exposed. Keep fibre moist at all times. Plant in the garden after flowering.

PROPAGATION Remove offsets when lifting bulbs in late spring.

CACTI AND SUCCULENTS

Agave americana
CENTURY PLANT

The century plant produces a large rosette of spine-edged, sword-like, greyish green leaves. There are cultivars with cream or yellow striped leaves. This succulent will not flower in pots.

TEMPERATURE   As for *Aloe.*

HUMIDITY   As for *Aloe.*

LIGHT   As for *Aloe.*

GENERAL CULTIVATION   As for *Aloe.*

PROPAGATION   Remove and pot offsets.

Aloe
ALOE

These easily grown succulent plants of the lily family are generally represented in the home by the partridge-breasted aloe (*A. variegata*). It produces a rosette of deep green triangular leaves, banded and spotted with white. The flowers are produced in spring, and vary in colour from pink to scarlet.

TEMPERATURE   Provide high temperatures in spring and summer, but in the resting period, from mid-autumn to early spring, provide a temperature of 7–10°C (45–50°F).

HUMIDITY   Dry air preferable.

LIGHT   Maximum light needed, and a position in full sun. These plants should

Left Among the most easily grown succulent plants are the aloes. This one is the popular partridge-breasted aloe, *A. variegata*, which flowers freely in the spring, over a long period

be grown on a sunny windowsill.

GENERAL CULTIVATION In the growing period water as required. Between mid-autumn and early spring keep dry, but if excessive shrivelling occurs then water may be given. Feed monthly in summer. Pot-on in spring as required, using a proprietary cactus compost. Do not use too large a pot.

PROPAGATION Remove and pot off-sets; or propagate from leaf cuttings.

Bryophyllum
BRYOPHYLLUM

Two species of these succulents are very popular because they produce tiny plantlets on the leaves. *B. daigremontianum* has triangular leaves and pink or yellow blooms. *B. tubiflorum* has thin cylindrical leaves and produces orange blooms. Easy room plants.

TEMPERATURE As for *Aloe*.

HUMIDITY As for *Aloe*.

LIGHT As for *Aloe*.

GENERAL CULTIVATION As for *Aloe*, but quite a rich compost is preferred.

PROPAGATION Remove plantlets and pot them up.

Chamaecereus silvestrii
PEANUT CACTUS

This very popular cactus has branching stems, composed of peanut-shaped sections. Orange or red flowers are produced in spring and summer.

TEMPERATURE As for *Aloe*.

HUMIDITY As for *Aloe*.

LIGHT As for *Aloe*.

GENERAL CULTIVATION As for *Aloe*.

PROPAGATION Take cuttings in spring or summer.

Crassula portulacea
JADE TREE

This tough, very easy-going succulent forms a branching shrub with thick, rounded leaves, mid-green and shiny. The jade tree does not usually produce flowers when pot grown.

TEMPERATURE As for *Aloe*.

HUMIDITY As for *Aloe*.

LIGHT As for *Aloe*.

GENERAL CULTIVATION As for *Aloe*.

PROPAGATION Take cuttings in spring or summer.

Epiphyllum
ORCHID CACTI

Epiphyllums are easy and free-flowering epiphytic, or tree-dwelling, cacti. The flat stems are jointed and leaf-like, and bear large cup- or trumpet-shaped blooms in summer in a very wide range of colours. Cactus nurseries can offer several hundred named cultivars and hybrids.

TEMPERATURE Provide a minimum of 10°C (50°F) during the autumn and winter, 18°C (65°F) and above for the rest of the year.

HUMIDITY High humidity needed in warm conditions, less in cool conditions.

LIGHT Provide maximum light in winter, but give light shade from sun from spring to autumn.

GENERAL CULTIVATION Provide plenty of fresh air. Use peat-based potting compost with extra coarse sand added. Pot-on in spring as required. Water plants throughout the year, allow-

Right The jade tree, or *Crassula portulacea*, is a tough, very easy-going succulent with a branching habit. When grown in pots it does not usually produce flowers

Left Orchid cacti flower very freely in the summer and come in a wide range of colours. In the wild they grow on trees and are, therefore, suited to elevated containers. These cacti like high humidity and warm conditions in summer

ing compost almost to dry out between applications. Feed in spring and summer, every two to three weeks. Avoid fluctuating temperatures, which can cause bud drop.

PROPAGATION Take cuttings (stem sections) in spring or summer.

Ferocactus
FEROCACTUS

This popular cactus has rounded or cylindrical, heavily spined stems. It is free-flowering with the blooms being red, yellow or violet. Various species are available, and all are worth growing.

TEMPERATURE As for *Aloe*.

HUMIDITY As for *Aloe*.

LIGHT As for *Aloe*.

GENERAL CULTIVATION As for *Aloe*, but likes a very well-drained compost and restrained watering.

PROPAGATION By seeds sown in spring.

Kalanchoe tomentosa
PANDA PLANT

This attractive succulent forms rosettes of green leaves, densely covered with short white hairs, rusty brown at the edges.

TEMPERATURE As for *Aloe*.

HUMIDITY As for *Aloe*.

LIGHT As for *Aloe*.

GENERAL CULTIVATION As for *Aloe*. Water sparingly even during the growing season.

PROPAGATION Cuttings and offsets are easily rooted in spring.

Lithops
LIVING STONES

As the common name suggests, these succulents resemble stones and pebbles. They come in various colours and patterns and produce yellow or white flowers. Basically the plants are composed of two swollen leaves; these

Above Lobivias are very popular cacti as they are easy to grow and flower very freely. The blooms may be red, orange or yellow, depending on the species or variety. All are worth growing

PROPAGATION   Sow seeds in spring.

Mammillaria
MAMMILLARIA

Mammillaria are one of the most popular groups of cacti, because they are easy to grow and free-flowering. Generally globular plants, or sometimes cylindrical, they are very prickly. The flowers are small and appear during the summer. They are usually yellow, but white and red forms are available.

TEMPERATURE   As for *Aloe*.

HUMIDITY   As for *Aloe*.

LIGHT   As for *Aloe*.

GENERAL CULTIVATION   As for *Aloe*.

PROPAGATION   Divide   clumps   or remove and pot-up offsets.

Notocactus
NOTOCACTUS

Easy and generally free-flowering, these cacti are usually globular with a flattish top, and very spiny. The flowers, which are mainly yellow, are large and appear in summer.

TEMPERATURE   As for *Aloe*.

HUMIDITY   As for *Aloe*.

LIGHT   As for *Aloe*.

GENERAL CULTIVATION   As for *Aloe*.

PROPAGATION   Remove   and   pot-up offsets in spring.

Rebutia
REBUTIA

These very popular, easy, free-flowering cacti are generally globular in shape. Trumpet-shaped red, orange, orange-red, or yellow flowers are produced in summer.

TEMPERATURE   As for *Aloe*.

HUMIDITY   As for *Aloe*.

LIGHT   As for *Aloe*.

shrivel in the winter rest period but new ones are produced in spring.

TEMPERATURE   As for *Aloe*.

HUMIDITY   As for *Aloe*.

LIGHT   As for *Aloe*.

GENERAL CULTIVATION   As for *Aloe*, but water sparingly, and never in the period mid-autumn to mid-spring.

PROPAGATION   Sow seeds or divide.

Lobivia
LOBIVIA

These popular cacti are round or cylindrical, and spiny. Very easy to grow, they are free-flowering, with red, orange or yellow blooms, depending on the species or hybrid.

TEMPERATURE   As for *Aloe*.

HUMIDITY   As for *Aloe*.

LIGHT   As for *Aloe*, but provide some shade from the hottest sun.

GENERAL CULTIVATION   As for *Aloe*, but a rich limy compost is preferred.

GENERAL CULTIVATION As for *Aloe*.

PROPAGATION Sow seeds or detach and pot-up offsets in spring.

Rhipsalidopsis gaertneri
EASTER CACTUS

The Easter cactus is similar to the Christmas cactus but flowers in spring. The blooms are scarlet. Like the Christmas cactus, this is an ideal subject for hanging containers.

TEMPERATURE As for *Epiphyllum*.

HUMIDITY As for *Epiphyllum*.

LIGHT As for *Epiphyllum*.

GENERAL CULTIVATION As for *Epiphyllum*.

PROPAGATION As for *Epiphyllum*.

Schlumbergera × buckleyi
CHRISTMAS CACTUS

This is a popular cactus which flowers at Christmastime, bearing magenta or deep pink flowers, on pendulous, flat, leaf-like joined stems. It is one of the forest cacti, living on trees in the wild.

TEMPERATURE As for *Epiphyllum*.

HUMIDITY As for *Epiphyllum*.

LIGHT As for *Epiphyllum*.

GENERAL CULTIVATION As for *Epiphyllum*.

PROPAGATION Take cuttings (stem sections) spring or summer.

Below This is one of the newer Christmas cacti, with bi-coloured flowers. They do, in fact, flower around Christmas time, and when the buds are forming the pot must not be turned or the buds may drop, as they grow towards the light

CHAPTER FIVE

SPECIAL WAYS
WITH HOUSEPLANTS

Opposite This unusual, rather squat bottle is attractive in itself but is large enough to hold quite a good collection of plants

Below All kinds of bottles are suitable for use as bottle gardens, provided the glass is clear

THERE IS NO NEED to grow all your houseplants in pots. There are several other ways of displaying them attractively: in bottle gardens, hanging containers, on wall trellis, and on a 'plant-tree'. Nor is there any need to grow all of them indoors all the year round, either: some can be placed out of doors for summer display, while bonsai (artificially dwarfed trees) are grown all year round in the open and taken inside for short spells only to create a special effect.

BOTTLE GARDENS

Some plants, particularly the more difficult kinds, can be grown in a large bottle such as a carboy or demi-john. In such a container they have their own micro-climate: a steady warm temperature, very humid conditions and freedom from draughts.

The idea of a totally closed container goes back to the Victorian Wardian case (see page 4), and today we use, apart from bottles, various other enclosed containers, including fish tanks, goldfish bowls and confectionary jars. They all come under the umbrella term 'bottle gardens' and all can make very attractive room features. The term 'bottle' has been used in this book to refer to other containers as well.

Choosing Plants

It is best to avoid using most flowering plants, because in many bottles it is difficult to remove dead flowers. Buy small plants as these are easier to get through narrow openings. Also choose only naturally small and slow-growing species — large, quick growers would rapidly fill a bottle.

Try some of the following: dwarf palms (e.g. *Chamaedorea elegans*), false aralia (*Dizygotheca*), earth stars (*Cryptanthus*), mosaic plant (*Fittonia*), prayer plant (*Maranta*), pepper elder (*Peperomia*), moss ferns (*Selaginella*), maidenhair ferns (*Adiantum*), *Begonia boweri*, flame

violet (*Episcia*), peacock plant (*Calathea*) and button fern (*Pellaea rotundifolia*).

Preparation and Planting

First, make sure the bottle is made of clear, not tinted, glass. Wash it out well with soapy water and allow to dry.

Place a layer of washed gravel in the bottom for drainage — in bottles with a narrow neck use a cardboard funnel to guide the gravel in. Then add a few pieces of charcoal to keep the compost 'sweet'. Place a layer of peat-based or soil-based potting compost over the gravel (again use a cardboard funnel) and firm with a cotton-reel on the end of a bamboo cane. The layers of gravel and compost should take up a quarter of the bottle space.

Before planting, arrange the plants outside the bottle — on a piece of paper the diameter of the container. This will ensure you create a pleasing design and also avoid using too many plants. Allow room for each one to grow; plants must not touch each other in the early stages. As a general rule, place taller plants in the centre and lower-growing ones near the sides of the container.

Remove most of the soil from around the roots if you are using a narrow-necked bottle, and start planting from the outside, working towards the centre. Planting holes can be made with a spoon tied to a bamboo cane. Plants can be held and lowered into the bottle with a wire ring attached to a cane. Cover the roots, using the spoon, and firm with your cotton-reel.

Water in the plants, but do not give too much, just sufficient to moisten the compost slightly (about a cupful of water for a carboy). Trickle the water down the sides of the bottle — this will also wash off any adhering compost — then replace the stopper or lid.

Condensation should form on the glass within a few days — if not, add a little more water. If condensation is excessive, however, remove the stopper or lid for a few days. Eventually a state of equilibrium will be reached and plants will then need watering very infrequently — a matter of several months between waterings — because the water is continually recycled.

It is important to remove any dead and dying leaves to prevent disease building up. Cut off leaves with a razor blade attached to a bamboo cane. Pick them up with a pointed cane.

Position your bottle garden out of direct sun; a north-facing windowsill is a good location.

Above Here a funnel and a cardboard tube are being used to add the gravel and potting compost

Below If necessary, larger plants can be protected with a cylinder of rolled paper as they are being lowered into place through narrow necks

Above Ingenious bamboo 'tweezers' being used to insert small plants. They can also be used for moving plants into their final positions in the bottle

Above Compost can be firmed around plants with a cotton reel on the end of a bamboo cane

HANGING CONTAINERS

There are various kinds of hanging containers that can be used for displaying trailing plants. The traditional galvanized-wire basket could be used if it is fitted with a drip tray, although this is really meant for outdoor displays. Plastic hanging baskets (the non-perforated type) are better and can be obtained with a built-in drip tray. Pottery containers on ropes (macramé work) are popular. Trailing plants are often sold in hanging plastic pots with built-in drip trays, complete with hanging equipment and all ready to hang up.

Strong hooks are needed for hanging containers, because some of them can be heavy. Ornamental wrought-iron brackets, for example, are very attractive.

Planting and Care

Only one kind of houseplant is usually planted in a hanging container, rather than several sorts together. If you are using a wire basket, first line it with

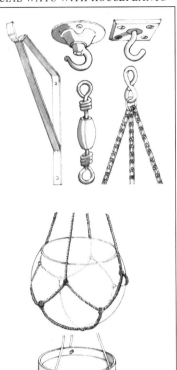

Above There are many kinds of hook and bracket available to support hanging containers, which are becoming very popular for indoor plant display. One can also find in garden centres a wide range of containers suitable for use indoors

Left This is the white form of the bellflower, or *Campanula isophylla*, a very popular plant for hanging containers in the cooler rooms of the house

Above There are plenty of trailing plants for hanging containers, including the wandering Jew or tradescantia. This plant is very tolerant of a wide range of conditions so the average home will have several suitable places for it

INDOOR TRELLIS

To make good use of indoor wall space, try displaying plants on indoor trellis. It is possible to buy from garden centres trellis panels of various shapes and sizes, often in plastic-coated steel. You can also buy pot holders which can be hooked onto the trellis, the plants being simply placed in them. Trellis comes complete with fixing brackets and is easily installed. Any of the trailing plants just listed can be used, and this is also a suitable way to display pot-grown bromeliads and the stag's horn fern (*Platycerium bifurcatum*).

HOUSEPLANTS OUTDOORS

Some houseplants can be grown out of doors for the summer, say in window boxes or in pots, urns and tubs on a patio or balcony. Often they are used in conjunction with summer bedding plants to create colourful combinations of flowes and foliage. Houseplants suitable for outdoor display include geraniums (*Pelargonium*), busy lizzies (*Impatiens*), hydrangeas, flame nettle (*Coleus*), ivies (*Hedera*), Japanese aralia (*Fatsia japonica*), pick-a-back plant (*Tolmiea menziesii*), spider plant (*Chlorophytum comosum* 'Variegatum'), and the century plant (*Agave americana*).

Some indoor plants particularly benefit from a spell outside from early summer to early autumn, not necessarily for display but to encourage them to make better growth and to ripen new growth. This results in better flowering. Plants treated in this way are azaleas (*Rhododendron*), regal pelargoniums (*Pelargonium domesticum*), Christmas cactus (*Schlumbergera* × *buckleyi*), Easter cactus (*Rhipsalidopsis gaertneri*), and orchid cacti (*Epiphyllum*).

BONSAI

Bonsai is the art of dwarfing trees artificially. The trees are grown in shallow containers to restrict root growth, and this is combined with regular root pruning and branch training. Bonsai literally means a plant in a tray or shallow container, and the technique was originally developed by the Chinese and Japanese.

sphagnum moss. Planting any container is straightforward: simply put a layer of potting compost in the bottom, lightly firm it, place the plant in the centre, and maybe a few around the edge if it is a large container, and trickle compost around the rootball and firm it. Leave a space of 12–25mm (½–1in) at the top to allow room for watering. Water well in after planting.

To provide humidity for hanging plants, mist spray them daily. Keep a close eye on the compost, too, for it can dry out rapidly.

Some Suitable Plants

There are many trailing houseplants which can be used, and also some climbers which can be allowed to trail. All the following are suitable and will be found described in Chapter Four.

Bellflower (*Campanula isophylla*), asparagus fern (*Asparagus densiflorus* 'Sprengeri'), devil's ivy (*Scindapsus aureus*), figs (*Ficus pumila* and *F. radicans* 'Variegata'), flame violet (*Episcia*), goose foot (*Syngonium podophyllum*), grape ivy (*Cissus rhombifolia*), ivy (*Hedera*), mother of thousands (*Saxifraga stolonifera*), *Philodendron scandens*, pick-a-back plant (*Tolmiea menziesii*), spider plant (*Chlorophytum comosum* 'Variegatum'), wandering Jew (*Tradescantia* and *Zebrina*), Christmas cactus (*Schlumbergera* × *buckleyi*), Easter cactus (*Rhipsalidopsis gaertneri*) and orchid cacti (*Epiphyllum*).

Buying and Uses

The majority of bonsai trees are hardy and therefore definitely not indoor plants. They are slow-growing trees which originate from temperate climates, so they must be grown out of doors and are particularly recommended for a balcony or patio. However, the plants can be brought indoors for short periods at a time — a week at the most — if you want to create some special effect. When the plants are inside they should be placed in a cool, airy room in maximum light, and should be sprayed once or twice a day with plain water, ideally with rain- or soft water.

You can buy bonsai from garden centres, some florists and also from specialist suppliers. They are expensive, and the older the tree the higher the price. In private collections there are trees 50 to 100 years or more old and these are worth a small fortune.

There are one or two points to watch out for when buying. Make sure the tree is really firm in its container. If it is loose it means that the roots are not anchored properly. The compost should be moist but not wet, and certainly not dry. The plant should look in good condition, with leaves bright and healthy.

You could perhaps produce your own bonsai trees from seeds, or from seedlings carefully dug up, but more of this later.

Suitable Bonsai Trees

You have a choice of evergreen or deciduous trees; the latter drop their leaves in the autumn. Popular evergreens are pine, juniper, spruce, cedar and yew. Deciduous small-leaved trees include maples (especially the Japanese maples), elm, hornbeam, beech and birch.

Flowering trees often used for bonsai include ornamental cherries, crab apples (these also produce fruits), pyracantha (these also produce red or orange berries), and thorns (*Crataegus*).

Below Bonsai trees can be brought indoors for short periods — say for a week at the most — perhaps when they are looking particularly attractive: maybe with autumn leaf tints as can be seen in some of these specimens

Training and Care

Bonsai trees can be trained in various traditional shapes: for example, informal upright (varies from the shape of a typical tree growing in a field to a naturally sloping pine), formal upright (the tree retains an upright habit with the branches well balanced around the trunk), cascade (the tree curves downwards so that most of the tree is below the level of the pot), and semi-cascade (where the tree is trained to grow almost horizontally).

Roots can be trained to grow over rocks, and this can look most attractive. So, too, can groups of trees grown to form a mini-forest. The ultimate size of the trees depends more on training and less on the species or type.

Containers specially for the cultivation of bonsai are available in muted or delicate colours, so they do not detract from the beauty of the plants. They must be frost-proof and glazed only on the outside. Of course, they must have drainage holes in the base. The depth of containers varies from 2.5 to 45cm (1 to 18in) and it is important that the size of the tree is balanced by the size of the pot.

The main method of training bonsai trees is by pruning. Wiring is a technique used to modify the shape and is fairly difficult (at least for beginners); it involves binding copper wire round various parts of the tree to bend it to a particular shape, and the wire is only removed when the plant can stand on its own in the selected position.

Pruning is much easier. It is carried out regularly but only a little at a time. The aim of pruning is to remove old wood, to shape the tree, to encourage budding, to remove unwanted branches and to encourage branches where you want them.

If branches are too long they are cut back to a suitable growth bud. If you want a branch to take on a new direction, cut it back just beyond a well-grown shoot.

Unnecessary branches, or those which confuse the overall shape, can be cut out. Traditional branches to remove are: those that are too low, those that directly oppose each other, and those that cross over the trunk.

Twigs are shortened, if necessary, to maintain a well-balanced tree.

Most pruning takes place in late winter, but flowering trees are pruned after flowering.

The initial training of seedlings needs great care. A seedling will have a large rootball and this should be pruned by half before planting in a container. Hold the rootball near the base of the trunk and break away the lower part of the soil. Prune back the roots in relation to the size of the tree and the container.

When planting, the trunk base must be firmly anchored to secure the tree in its container.

Loop wire through a two-holed container, or wrap it round a piece of cane under the dish for a one-holed container. Then secure the wire over the main roots at the base of the trunk. Use a soil-based compost and plant really firmly.

Apart from pruning and training, general care of bonsai consists of keeping the compost steadily moist. Never allow it to dry out and make sure it is not saturated with water. Keep your trees in an open sunny place as most do not like shade.

Below Various traditional shapes for bonsai trees: 1. An informal upright tree supported with a cane. 2. An oblique or semi-cascade, trained by twisting thick wire around the trunk. 3. A tree in the cascade style, tied down during the training process. 4. and 5. Branches are wired to change their direction of growth

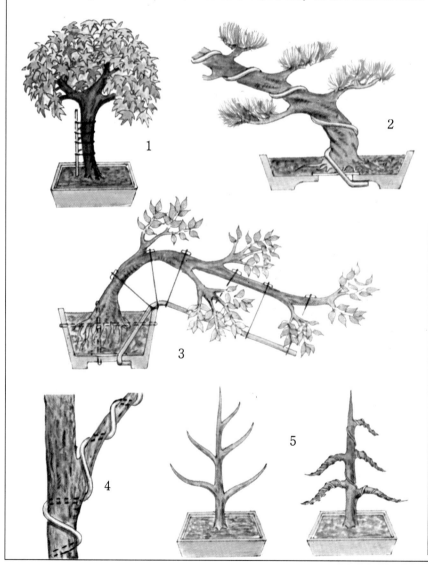

This is only a brief account of growing bonsai. There is much more to this fascinating art, and if you want more information, then refer to one of the several books available on this subject. Also visit specialist bonsai nurseries, and study the bonsai exhibits and competitions at flower shows. There is even a bonsai society that you could join if you become really keen on the subject.

PLANT-TREE

A fascinating, highly decorative and very practical way to display epiphytic plants (those that grow naturally on trees) is to grow them on a plant-tree. This is very popular in America and the idea is catching on now in the U.K.

Plants to grow on a tree include the smaller kinds of bromeliads (larger ones are more difficult to secure), including the atmospheric tillandias or air plants; the Christmas and Easter cacti and the orchid cacti. It is best to start off with small plants as they are much easier to mount. As they grow they will start to support themselves.

Making a Plant-Tree

First you will need a reasonably thick, well-shaped branch from a dead tree. The more this is forked the better, for not only does it look more attractive, but plants are more easily mounted as they can be gently wedged in the crotches. Try to find a branch with the bark still intact, as this looks more natural, and make sure it is not starting to rot. The size is up to you — you could have a small tree, around 60–90cm (2–3ft) high, or one up to the ceiling, but bear in mind you may need to move it when the plants are sprayed and watered.

For most people, obtaining a suitable

branch means scouring the countryside for dead, fallen branches. On no account, though, cut off branches from trees in the countryside. You may well come across a tree surgeon in your area who is removing some branches from a tree — there would be no harm in asking for one.

Having obtained a suitable branch, the next step is to make it stand upright. This is most easily achieved by cementing it in a clay flower pot of suitable size. The branch should be tied or wedged in the desired position until the cement has set. Use a mortar mix of one part cement to four parts of builders' sand by volume.

When securing plants to the tree, remove them from their pots and tease away some of the compost from around the roots — to reduce the size of the rootball. This does not apply, of course, to the atmospheric tillandsias, which are never grown in pots.

Surround the roots with sphagnum moss to retain the remaining compost, and tie the plant to the tree with thin

Left The stem of this bonsai juniper has been wired to create a twisted trunk. Junipers are among the most popular conifers for bonsai

Below Bromeliads growing on a moss-covered pole. They can also be grown on a plant-tree – made from a reasonably thick, well-shaped branch from a dead tree. The more this is forked the better will be the final appearance

Opposite The coleus, or flame nettle, is a short-term pot plant with leaves in many bright colours, depending on variety. It is best to raise new plants from seeds or cuttings each year because old ones are not as attractive as young specimens and tend to become leggy

Right Philodendrons are ideal plants for growing up moss poles. Their aerial roots will eventually grow into the moss, which should be kept moist

nylon string or thin plastic-coated wire. Make sure the roots and the base of the plant are secure: you may need one or two more ties higher up. Do not tie tightly, and try to make the ties as inconspicuous as possible.

If you have a well-branched tree, there may be no need to tie on some of the plants, as they could be gently wedged in the crotches of the branches.

Another method of securing plants is to make 'pockets' on the tree with pieces of bark, or cork bark, suitably nailed in place. These pockets can then be filled with compost and the plants positioned in this.

Remember that the atmospheric tillandsias, or air plants, do not need compost or moss around their roots (if indeed they have any); they are simply tied or wedged onto the tree as they are. The Spanish moss (*Tillandsia usneoides*) can simply be hung over a branch.

When you have planted your tree, it should be stood in a suitable place for the conditions required by the plants: refer to Chapter Four. To water the plants the whole tree is syringed or sprayed with water, and to do this you may need to take it outside or into the bathroom or kitchen. For water requirements, again refer to the appropriate plants in Chapter Four.

MOSS POLES

A very attractive way of displaying and supporting certain climbing plants is to grow them up moss poles. The plants like this system, too, for they have abundant moisture and something for their aerial roots to grow into. Indeed, this method is best suited to plants which produce aerial roots (roots from the stems), like philodendrons, Swiss cheese plants, etc.

You can buy moss poles from garden centres, in various lengths, but it is very easy to make your own and in any case they are much better than many ready-made poles.

Making a Moss Pole

You will need a broom handle of suitable length: the length will depend on the final height you wish your plant to attain.

The moss pole is formed in a pot, and then the climber is planted. Insert the broom handle into a pot of compost, with the base touching the bottom of the pot.

Firm the compost well to support it.

Over the pole, place a wire-netting cylinder, using small-mesh wire netting. This can be up to two or three times the diameter of the broom handle. The netting cylinder should extend below the surface of the compost.

Now pack the cylinder with live sphagnum moss, which you should be able to obtain from a florist or garden centre. It is best to use live moss, as it then keeps growing and stays an attractive green colour. The moss is simply pushed through the wire mesh until the cylinder is full and well packed.

In order to moisten the moss easily — it should be kept moist at all times — insert a plastic pot of suitable size in the top of the pole, so that it rests on top of the broom handle and the rim is level with the top of the wire netting. This pot is then filled with water when you want to moisten the moss, and the water will trickle down through the moss. You may need to mist spray the outside of the pole as well.

Once the moss pole is completed, plant your climber, preferably using a small young specimen so there is not too much upheaval of the compost. The plant may need some initial support by being tied to the pole with garden string, but once aerial roots start to grow into the moss, it will support itself. If necessary carefully guide aerial roots into the moss, for some are inclined to grow straight down to the compost on the outside of the pole.

INDEX

Acknowledgements

The publishers would like to thank Squire's Garden Centre, Twickenham and The Chelsea Gardener, Sydney Street, London SW3 for supplying plants and equipment for the cover photograph.

Picture credits
Bernard Alfieri: 34, 48, 50 (r)
Steve Bicknell: 57 (t), 60, 64, 74
Michael Boys: 11, 16, 41, 85 (t)
Pat Brindley: Frontispiece, 2/3, 7, 29, 42, 44 (l), 45 (t), 46, 50 (l), 51, 53, 58 (t, br), 59, 71, 72, 73, 75, 78
Mary Evans: 6 (t)
Valerie Finnis: 20
John Glover: Endpapers
Derek Gould: 87
Naru Inui: 24
Dave Kelly: 86
Peter McHoy: 85 (b)
John Melville: 17 (t), 40, 55 (b), 62, 63, 68, 70, 82
Harry Smith Horticultural Photographic Collection: 6 (b), 8, 9, 13, 14 (t), 17 (b), 18, 19, 23, 25, 35, 39, 43, 44 (r), 45 (b), 47, 49 (b), 52, 54, 55 (t), 56, 58 (bl), 61, 67, 69, 76, 77, 81, 83
Pamla Toler: 4, 14 (b)
Jerry Tubby: 12
Colin Watmough: 49 (t)
Elizabeth Whiting: 5, 15

Line artwork
Richard Phipps: 30, 31, 32, 33, 34, 35